Δ The Triangle Papers: 49

GLOBALIZATION AND TRILATERAL LABOR MARKETS: EVIDENCE AND IMPLICATIONS

A Report to
The Trilateral Commission

Authors: NIELS THYGESEN
Professor of Economics, Economics Institute,
University of Copenhagen

YUTAKA KOSAI
President,
Japan Center for Economic Research

ROBERT Z. LAWRENCE
Professor of International Trade and Investment,
Kennedy School of Government,
Harvard University

published by
The Trilateral Commission
New York, Paris and Tokyo
December 1996

n 1973 by private citizens of Western
er closer cooperation among these three
democratic industrialized regions on common problems. It seeks to improve public
understanding of such problems, to support proposals for handling them jointly,
and to nurture habits and practices of working together among these regions.

Library of Congress Cataloging-in-Publication Data

Thygesen, Niels
    Globalization and Trilateral Labor Markets: Evidence and
Implications: a report to the Trilateral Commission/authors:
Niels Thygesen, Yutaka Kosai, Robert Z. Lawrence
        p. cm. — (The Triangle papers: 49)

    Includes bibliographical references (p. 110).
    ISBN 0-930503-74-0

1. Foreign trade and employment. 2. Labor market. 3. International
trade. 4. Wages. 5. Unemployment. 6. Foreign trade and
employment—United States. 7. Foreign trade and
employment—Japan. 8. Foreign trade and employment—European
Union countries. I. Kosai, Yutaka, 1933- . II. Lawrence, Robert Z.,
1949- . III. Title. IV. Series.

HD5710.7.T49 1996
331.12—dc21
                                                                96-50188
                                                                    CIP

Manufactured in the United States of America

THE TRILATERAL COMMISSION

345 East 46th Street   c/o Japan Center for   35, avenue de Friedland
New York, NY 10017   International Exchange   75008 Paris, France
                                          4-9-17 Minami-Azabu
                                                Minato-ku
                                                Tokyo, Japan

The Authors

NIELS THYGESEN is Professor of Economics at the Economics Institute of Copenhagen University, where he has been teaching since 1971. He has had very wide international experience, including service as head of the Monetary Division of the OECD Secretariat in Paris, on several expert groups set up by the European Communities, and as Economic Advisor to the Ministry of Finance of Malaysia and to the Government of Sweden. He has been a board member of the European University Institute and of the A.P. Moller Shipping Line; and he was Vice Chairman of the Novo Foundation. Professor Thygesen was an independent member of the Delors Committee for the Study of Economic and Monetary Union in Europe, to which he was nominated by the European Council in 1988. His publications include *European Monetary Integration* (with Daniel Gros, 1992).

YUTAKA KOSAI is President of the Japan Center for Economic Research. He earned his B.A. (economics, 1958) from the University of Tokyo and M.A. (economics, 1967) from Stanford University. From 1958 to 1981 he served in the Planning Bureau of the Economic Planning Agency (EPA). He was Director of EPA's Office of Research on the System of National Accounts in 1973–76; Director of the Industrial Economic Affairs Division in 1976–78; and Director of the Price Coordination Division in 1978–80. Mr. Kosai was a Professor at the Tokyo Institute of Technology from 1981 until assuming his present position in 1987. His publications include *The Contemporary Japanese Economy* (1984), *The Era of High-Speed Growth* (1986) and *The Japanese Experience of Economic Reforms* (1993). He was awarded the Suntory Gakugeisho in 1980, the Nikkei Keizai Tosho Bunkasho in 1981 and the Ohira Kinensho in 1994.

ROBERT Z. LAWRENCE is Albert L. Williams Professor of International Trade and Investment at the Kennedy School of Government at Harvard University and a Research Associate at the National Bureau of Economic Research. Prof. Lawrence is also a Non-Resident Senior Fellow of the Brookings Institution, where he was on the Economic Studies Program staff in 1976-90. Along with Albert Bressand and Takatoshi Ito, he authored *A Vision for the World Economy* (1996), the capstone volume of the recently completed Brookings-led project on Integrating National Economies. Among his recent publications in the area of this report are *The Impact of Trade on OECD Labor Markets* (Group of Thirty Occasional Paper, 1994) and a new book entitled *Single World Divided Nations: International Trade and OECD Labor Markets* (Brookings and the OECD Development Centre, 1996).

The Trilateral Process

The report which follows is the responsibility of its three authors, with Niels Thygesen serving as lead author. Niels Thygesen drafted the introductory and concluding chapters, and the Europe chapter. Robert Lawrence drafted the chapter focused on the United States. The chapter on Japan was written by Yutaka Kosai in collaboration with Reiko Suzuki and Yukiko Ito, colleagues of his at the Japan Center for Economic Research.

This project grew out of discussions among the Chairmen and Executive Committee members in late 1994 and early 1995, including in the wings of the April 1995 annual meeting in Copenhagen. The authors were chosen in the spring and summer of 1995 and held their first meeting at Harvard in late September 1995 to establish the broad outline and thrusts of the report. The authors met again in Paris in early 1996—at the end of January and beginning of February—to discuss first drafts of some chapters and review the arguments of other chapters. A full draft was discussed at the Commission's 1996 annual meeting in Vancouver on April 20-22.

The consultations for this report were concentrated in Europe. Along with consulting at the European Commission in Brussels and several times at the OECD in Paris, Niels Thygesen discussed the report with Trilateral Commission members and others in Milan on February 27, in London on March 12, and in Cologne on March 26. All three authors consulted with French Trilateral members and others, including OECD experts, when they met in Paris early in 1996.

Only the authors are responsible for their analysis and conclusions. The persons consulted spoke as individuals and not for any institutions with which they are associated. The persons consulted or otherwise assisting in the preparation of this report include:

Michel Albert, *Membre de l'Institut de France; Member of the Council for Monetary Policy of the Banque de France, Paris; Honorary Chairman, Assurances Générales de France*
Piero Bassetti, *Chairman, Chamber of Commerce and Industry of Milan; former Member of Chamber of Deputies*
Enrico Beneduce, *Chief Executive Officer, COMIT*
Georges Berthoin, *International Honorary Chairman, European Movement; Honorary European Chairman, The Trilateral Commission, Paris*
Carlo Boffito, *Professor at the University of Turin*

Giorgio Brechet, *General Director, Istituto Mobiliare Italiano*
Franco Bruni, *Co-Director, Scientific Committee of ISPI*
Pierre-André Buigues, *Head of Unit, General Directorate for Economic and Financial Affairs, European Commission, Brussels*
Hervé de Carmoy, *Chairman, Banque Industrielle et Mobilière Privée, Paris; former Chief Executive, Société Générale de Belgique, Brussels*
Fausto Cereti, *Chairman, Alitalia, Rome*
Alain Cotta, *Professor of Economics and Management, University of Paris*
Mario Deaglio, *Professor at the University of Turin*
Jean Deflassieux, *Chairman, Banque des Echanges Internationaux; Honorary Chairman, Crédit Lyonnais, Paris*
Nadio Delai, *Director for Economic & Social Affairs, Ferrovie dello Stato (Italian State Railways)*
Joergen Elmeskov, *Counsellor, Structural Policy, OECD, Paris*
Bill Emmott, *Editor,* The Economist, *London*
Gerhard Fels, *Managing Director, Institut der Deutschen Wirtschaft, Cologne; Member of the Group of Thirty; Professor of Economics, University of Cologne*
Tristan Garel-Jones, *Member of British Parliament; former Minister of State at the Foreign Office (European Affairs)*
John Gilbert, *Member of British Parliament; former Treasury, Transport and Defence Minister; Chairman of John Gilbert & Associates, London*
Marcello Guidi, *Chairman, ISPI, Milan; former Ambassador of Italy*
Renate Hornung-Draus, *Director for International and European Social Policy, Confederation of German Employers' Associations (BDA), Cologne*
Alexis Jacquemin, *Principal Advisor to the General Directorate for Science, Research and Development; European Commission, Brussels*
Charles B. Heck, *North American Director, Trilateral Commission*
Sir Michael Jenkins, *Vice Chairman, Kleinwort Benson Group, London; former British Ambassador*
Alain Joly, *Chairman and Chief Executive Officer, L'Air Liquide, Paris*
Lawrence F. Katz, *Professor of Economics, Harvard University; former Chief Economist, U.S. Department of Labor*
Pier Carlo Marengo, *Chairman, Servizi Interbancari*
John P. Martin, *Deputy Director for Education, Employment, Labour and Social Affairs, OECD, Paris*
Patrick Messerlin, *Professor, Institute of Political Studies, Paris*
Thierry de Montbrial, *Membre de l'Institut de France; Professor, Ecole Polytechnique; Director, French Institute for International Relations (IFRI), Paris*

Aldo Montesano, *Co-Dean, Bocconi University*
Klaus Murmann, *Chairman, Confederation of German Employers' Associations (BDA), Cologne*
Makito Noda, *Senior Program Officer, Japan Center for International Exchange*
Romano Pesci, *Deputy Director General, Cassa di Risparmio delle Provincia Lombarde*
Paul Révay, *European Director, Trilateral Commission*
Axel Rhein, *Economist, Institut der Deutschen Wirtschaft, Cologne*
Lord Roll of Ipsden, *President, S.G. Warburg Group, London*
Sergio Romano, *Editorialist,* La Stampa; *former Italian Ambassador to the USSR*
Claus Schnabel, *Senior Economist, Institut der Deutschen Wirtschaft, Cologne*
Peter Shore, *Member of British Parliament*
Umberto Silvestri, *Chairman, Telecom Italia, Rome*
Sir David Simon, *Chairman, BP, London*
Paul de Sury, *Professor, Bocconi University*
Sir Peter Tapsell, *Member of British Parliament*
Renata Targetti Lenti, *Professor, Bocconi and Pavia Universities*
Nick Vanston, *Head, Resources Allocation Division, OECD, Paris*
Ernesto Vellano, *Secretary-Treasurer of the Italian Group of the Trilateral Commission, Turin*
Reinhold Weiss, *Vice Head of the Education and Societal Studies Department, Institut der Deutschen Wirtschaft, Cologne*
Alan Lee Williams, *Director, The British Atlantic Council; former Member of British Parliament*
Peter Witte, *Assistant to the North American Director, Trilateral Commission*
Otto Wolff von Amerongen, *Chairman, East Committee of the German Industry; Chairman and Chief Executive Officer, Otto Wolff Industrieberatung und Beteiligung, Cologne*
Tadashi Yamamoto, *Japanese Director, Trilateral Commission; President, Japan Center for International Exchange*

Table of Contents

List of Figures and Tables

I. Introduction

Over the post-war period international trade and investment flows have expanded steadily and rapidly, helped by the gradual lowering of tariffs and other barriers to trade, by liberalization of the regime for investment flows, and by the dramatic fall in the cost of transportation and communication. These trends helped the industrial countries to overcome the rupture in international economic relations caused by the inward-looking policies of the interwar period and the Second World War. Over the 30-40 years after 1945, the share of trade in the national economies of the industrial countries recovered to the levels observed in the beginning of the century—or beyond in some cases.

Growth of domestic economies and internationalization went hand in hand and came to be regarded as mutually reinforcing. Internationalization was therefore not regarded as controversial. This was true even in the early postwar period when large discrepancies in income and cost levels might have been regarded as upsetting and unfair; wages in Germany and Japan in the late 1940s were no higher as a fraction of U.S. wages than are the relative wages of many developing countries today compared to wages in the OECD countries. To its great credit the United States did not then insist on the prior establishment of a "level playing field" before giving the low-cost producers access to the U.S. market. Quite apart from the political benefits from vigorous trade and investment flows, growth was for a long time so rapid in Europe and Japan that the United States also benefitted.

The growth of trade between industrial countries has occasionally become a source of conflict when import penetration in exposed sectors became particularly rapid, or if trade imbalances appeared difficult to contain. Examples of such conflicts have been observed not least in trade between Japan and other industrial countries. But on the whole, concern in the public debate over these trade issues has been limited and the net benefit of a liberal trading regime among the industrial countries has not been fundamentally questioned. Within regions, integration of goods markets has deepened in the European Union and between Canada and the United States as a result of advances over the past decade in setting up the EU Single Market and a free trade area between Canada and the United States.

In the course of the 1980s, new countries, particularly in East Asia, joined in the internationalization process. Trade and investment flows with them grew at a faster pace than anything experienced within the OECD area and at times import penetration became so rapid that trade conflicts arose. But the aggregate effects were limited since trade volumes were still small—and the perception among consumers in the industrial countries that these major new suppliers (with highly favorable price/quality characteristics) provided clear benefits limited an incipient backlash towards trade with these Asian economies or direct investment flows from industrial countries to them.

A. THE CHALLENGE OF
A TRULY GLOBALIZED ECONOMY

Recently, the expansion of trade with the non-OECD area has become increasingly controversial. It proved just possible, nevertheless, to conclude the Uruguay Round in 1994 (hence continuing the trend towards lower tariffs of several earlier rounds of global trade negotiations) and to set up a World Trade Organization (with stronger powers than its predecessor, the GATT, to monitor infringements of agreed practices). Steps were also taken to phase out some quantitative restrictions the growth of which had, in the view of many observers, tended to largely offset over the 1970s and 1980s the effects of gradual cuts in tariffs (see Bhagwati [1990]). But the political will to pursue global trade liberalization has met with stronger resistance than have the efforts to deepen regional integration and facilitate the growth of trade among the industrial countries in general.

The reasons for this difference in attitude are not difficult to identify. Over the past few years large and populous states have entered the world economy in a way that was impossible to foresee even a decade ago. China, India, the countries of Central and Eastern Europe and of the former Soviet Union, and a number of others (e.g., Bangladesh, Vietnam, and several Latin American countries)—representing collectively more than 4 billion people— are in a process of rapid and far-reaching reform of their economic and political systems which may enable them to become major participants in a truly globalized economy. This is a far more dramatic challenge to the industrial countries than anything experienced in recent decades. The impressive performance of the so-called Dynamic Asian Economies (DAEs)—Hong Kong, South Korea, Malaysia, Singapore, Taiwan and Thailand, with a combined population of less than 150 million—has become very visible in trade with the industrial countries. Not only is the next wave of participants potentially very much more significant, but the initial discrepancy in cost levels is greater, prompting widespread fears of a levelling down of wages globally towards a world average way below the standards to which even the poorest presently industrialized countries have become accustomed.

Global Equalization of Wages?

Both dimensions of the apparent challenge are captured in Figure I-1 which shows average wages and population size for a number of countries. It is no surprise that many in the public debate in the Trilateral countries now see trade with the new, low-cost producers as both quantitatively important and potentially highly destructive of employment prospects at home at anything like the wages to which industrial country workers have become accustomed. These alarmist views argue that with today's high capital mobility the destructive features could manifest themselves quickly.

There are a number of reasons why the ominously suggestive nature of this challenge of global equalization of wages should not be taken at face value. Industrial country wages are not about to be determined in Beijing, to give a first answer to the question put in a recent article on globalization (see Freeman [1995]). The tendency for factor prices, in particular wages, to become equalized internationally is subject to a number of qualifications.

First, labor is not homogenous; better qualifications command a return to the human capital accumulated which protects many workers in traditional industrial countries from a levelling down of their pay. *Second,* protection against this trend is also offered by the way in which capital is used within the firm and in the society in which it operates. Better physical infrastructure, including communications and easy access to R&D, can keep up higher rewards to other factors of production. *Third,* to the extent that traditional industrial countries and their new trading partners have specialized fully in the production of different goods there is no further pressure for reducing wages in the former. *Fourth,* when the new economies enter the global trading system, wages in their internationally active

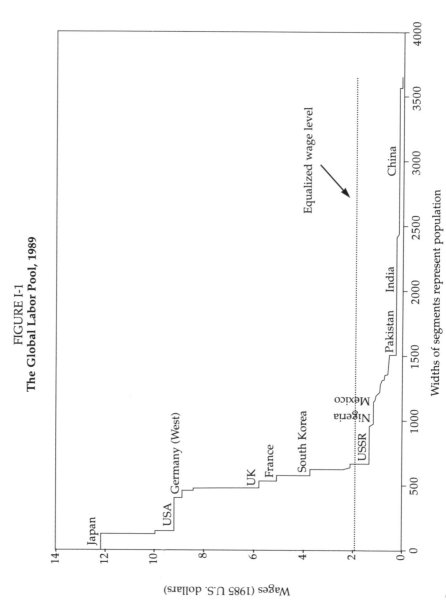

FIGURE I-1
The Global Labor Pool, 1989

Source: Leamer (1995), p. 40

sectors are likely to be bid up rapidly, as experience with the DAEs who have become major traders has shown. *Fifth*, trade flows with new, low-cost producers are likely to remain both modest for a long time relative to the size of the Trilateral economies and balanced, since the newcomers are likely to use all their export earnings to purchase goods and services in the OECD area.

Comparative Advantage Drives Mutually Beneficial Trade Flows

These qualifications may not greatly impress those who hold alarmist views of the issue. Some of these critics seem to stick to an older view of what determines trade, viz. that firms in countries with high wages can be outcompeted in all areas of production by low-cost newcomers. If the hourly wage is, say, US$15 in an OECD country and US$1 in China or Vietnam, no one would, according to this popular view, want to produce anything in the former. But starting with Ricardo's analysis of comparative advantage nearly two centuries ago, it has been recognized that trade flows are determined by the *relative* costs of producing different goods inside each trading country. The opening of trade permits each trading partner to shift resources into the sectors in which it has a comparative, or relative, advantage vis-à-vis its trading partners, hence specializing in ways that are not possible under autarky. A country with high costs in all sectors of its economy would still be able to export to lower-cost trading partners those goods in which it was relatively least inefficient, hence leaving scope for increasing living standards for workers and others engaged in domestic production.

A more sophisticated attack on comparative advantage as the main factor shaping trade flows starts from the observation that today's rapid dissemination of technological advances and, in particular, the vastly increased scope for shifting production processes to low-cost areas—usually labelled "delocalization"—have eroded whatever comparative advantage the industrial countries have historically enjoyed, with the exception of advantages linked to the availability of natural resources. When production processes can be shifted fairly rapidly, using the most advanced technology available, comparative advantage, even when accumulated steadily over long periods of time, can not be regarded as having been acquired once and for all, but is subject to a risk of sudden disappearance. The central idea in this modern version of the "pauperization hypothesis" is that workers in a low-cost country can almost overnight approach the levels of output-per-hour-worked observed in a high-cost country. Capital mobility, particularly when it takes the form of large-scale foreign direct investment, can make comparative advantage shift so rapidly that the notion becomes almost meaningless.

It is true—as one of the most vigorous proponents of this view, Sir James Goldsmith (1995), has noted—that traditional trade theory based on comparative advantage did not envisage the degree of capital mobility which has recently been observed. Having written about factors which tend to keep capital at home—primarily uncertainty and unfamiliarity with a foreign environment—Ricardo (1817) concluded (p. 155) that such factors

> induce most men of property to be satisfied with a low rate of profits in their own country, rather than seek a more advantageous employment for their wealth in foreign nations.

This perspective on international corporate behavior does indeed appear outdated in today's world where corporate managers have largely overcome earlier unfamiliarity with foreign environments and have become capable of comparing direct production costs in many different locations. In these circumstances the availability of local capital is no longer a constraint on the exploitation of comparative advantage by a new trading partner.

If one thinks of the process of globalization as one in which countries compete internationally by attracting mobile factors of production in order to combine them with their more or less immobile domestic factors in the most profitable way, the much wider scope for delocalization of production processes which liberalizing economic reforms in a number of new economies have made possible over the past decade marks a qualitative change. But this correct observation does not invalidate the general applicability of the principle of comparative advantage. The Trilateral countries are not about to be outcompeted in all or most traditional manufacturing activities because they have lost earlier and long-standing locational advantages on a massive scale. They have no doubt lost such advantages in an important degree in some sectors—textiles and toys are examples of industries where foreign direct investment has combined with particular ease with a local, low-cost labor force—but not in others, where new opportunities for exploiting comparative advantage have arisen because of wider markets in the new economies, for example for machinery or other relatively sophisticated products in the production of which the new economies typically find themselves at a competitive disadvantage.

The crucial point is that delocalization does not invalidate the traditional view, based on comparative advantage, of international trade as mutually beneficial for the parties involved, as long as differences between the trading partners persist. We already referred to human capital embodied in the labor force and to infrastructure (including communications) in our earlier dismissal of the belief in absolute advantage as the basis for trade. More broadly, one could speak not only of human capital, but also of social capital as immobile factors which form an important part of the comparative advantage which the Trilateral countries will continue to enjoy after their technological lead, more narrowly defined, has been eroded. These factors are only to a very limited extent mobile, although they can obviously be acquired—at a slow pace—by the new trading partners. We are left with a reformulated, but basically intact principle of comparative advantage as a basis for mutually advantageous trade.

There is a simpler way of expressing this point. If it were true that the diffusion of technology, mainly through foreign direct investment, is in itself sufficient to bring the productivity of labor in the new economies nearly to the level observed in the industrial countries while wages remain only a fraction of those in the latter, production in the new economies would provide massive returns to other factors of production and the catch-up in average income would be much faster than even the present impressive rate. But with some rare exceptions, the productivity of labor in the low-cost countries is not yet—for the reasons outlined above—anywhere near parity with productivity in the industrial countries, so the rewards to other factors of production (to be met out of the margin between the price of a product and the unit labor cost of producing it) are only moderately in excess of similar rewards in the industrial countries.

Relative Wages of Less-Skilled Workers

The conclusion of classical trade theory that the opening of trade is in the aggregate beneficial to both parties does not, however, imply that all categories of incomes will rise as trade expands. In a celebrated article Stolper and Samuelson (1941) showed that the opening of trade will benefit the factors of production used relatively intensively in the production of goods which find new outlets in foreign markets, but that it will lower the income of the factors of production used relatively intensively in the production of imported goods. If we think, as appears realistic, of the main imports from the new economies into the Trilateral countries as produced with relatively intensive use of unskilled labor (with which the former countries are amply endowed), then the growth of trade may reduce wages for unskilled workers in the Trilateral countries in the process of some levelling of wages between the two groups of countries. The precise nature of this levelling process is determined by some of the caveats mentioned above which prevent any full equalization of wages. Full equalization presupposes, in addition to the homogeneity of factors of production across frontiers, perfectly competitive markets. If one allows for the more realistic assumption that markets are less than perfectly competitive and that some firms or sectors earn rents because they are or have been particularly innovative, or simply are concentrated enough to exercise market power, there can be major departures from the tendency towards the factor price equalization predicted by pure theory. Strongly organized labor in some industries or centralized national wage bargaining may also be able to extract significant rents for their members over extended periods in otherwise increasingly exposed firms. A priori one would therefore expect industries characterized by a high degree of concentration and strong labor unions to exhibit the largest and the most long-lived escapes from factor price equalization.

Such sectoral privileges will obviously be eroded faster once trade with low-cost competitors expands in a major way, accelerated by foreign direct investments in new plants in their countries. So the factors that can account for major and long-lived departures from factor price equalization are themselves subject to gradual erosion, because the expansion of trade brings markets closer to the competitive pattern on which the theoretical paradigm is built. In the following chapters we therefore look both at the operation of competitive factor and product markets and at the erosion of rents in less competitive sectors.

Trade Inside and Outside the OECD Area: Intra-Industry and Inter-Industry Trade

To some extent all international trade flows—those among industrial countries and those between industrial countries and new trading partners—give rise to similar effects: increasing competitive pressures and more rapid erosion of privileged positions in traditionally well-sheltered industries. One should therefore expect similar attitudes politically and economically to the larger trade flows that have developed over a long period inside the OECD area and, with greater intensity, within regional trading arrangements (of which the

European Union is the prime example). Yet the expansion of intra-OECD trade meets with much less opposition from management and labor, and the general verdict that the process is welfare-enhancing and should be pursued further is rarely openly questioned by policymakers. In contrast, the rapid expansion of trade—from a very low starting point—with competitors outside the OECD area gives rise to concern and frequent efforts to slow down the process through the imposition of non-tariff barriers (such as so-called Voluntary Export Restraints [VERs]), lengthy transition periods for the implementation of trade agreements, etc.

From a purely economic point of view there is a puzzle. Trade theory expects any expansion of trade to improve aggregate welfare, even—with some less significant exceptions—in situations where liberalization is unilateral. The more different are the factor endowments of the trading partners, the greater the potential gains. This is particularly easy to see when trade with new partners opens up new consumption possibilities, because some of the goods imported could not be produced at all, or only at exorbitant cost, in the home country. But the overall net benefit of new trade should also be evident when some goods hitherto produced at home can be imported at significantly lower prices, hence raising the real income of domestic consumers, while the fall in output in the industries which meet new competitors is compensated by enlarged export possiblities for other industries. This latter effect is based on the observation that on the whole new trading partners will need to let their imports rise in step with, or even faster than, their own rapidly rising exports, rather than allow themselves to build up international reserves through large trade surpluses. The recent experience of the OECD countries has been that the rapid growth of the economies outside the OECD area, in combination with balanced trade, helped them to recover earlier from the recession of the early 1990s than they could have done strictly by their own efforts. This experience, with the degree of integration which already exists, should have helped to drive home the point that it would be harmful to the welfare of the industrial countries themselves to slow down trade expansion with the new economies.

The puzzle why this conclusion is not more generally recognized (despite being fairly robust to changes in particular circumstances as long as one looks at the OECD countries as a whole, because it is for this group that the prediction of balanced trade expansion with the non-OECD area can be most confidently asserted) is partly resolved when it is recognized that trade expansion produces both losers and winners and that redistribution to compensate the former can not be assumed to take care of itself without some form of government intervention in the individual industrial country. (We briefly discuss some possible interventions in Chapter V.) The perception that trade expansion brings national benefits in excess of the costs would also be fostered if competitive conditions within the group of industrial countries were sufficiently stable and balanced to assure a fair distribution of the net total benefits within the OECD area. If that is not the case (either because some industrial countries have achieved a major, though possibly temporary, improvement in competitiveness due to large depreciations of their currency, or because some industrial countries are for geographical, political or cultural reasons—maybe simply because of their size—clearly better placed to take advantage of expanding trade opportunities with new partners), trade liberalization is bound to be resisted by those countries which see themselves as least well-placed.

For each industrial country there is the problem of making it clear to its domestic electorate not only that the many who benefit from trade expansion (mainly through the lower prices to consumers of a range of imported goods) could compensate the relatively few who lose (because at a minimum their earnings are squeezed by the entry of low-cost competitors or, ultimately, because their jobs simply disappear), but also that steps have actually been taken to soften the impact imposed on the losers—without impeding the adjustment to the increasing trade flows.

Efforts at domestic redistribution are unquestionably more difficult in the case of trade expansion with new low-cost producers than in the more familiar case of deepening specialization among the industrial countries or within regional groupings of such countries. The greater difficulty is explained by the difference between the expansion of trade in basically similar products and of trade based on major differences in factor endowments and cost levels and entirely new producers taking advantage of large cost differences. The growth of trade among the industrial countries, and particularly within the European Union and the two industrial economies of North America, can be shown to be primarily of the former kind, so-called *intra-industry trade*. Here the gains come from increasing specialization within each industry, which makes possible the realization of economies of scale in the firms which survive. The crucial point is that most countries retain some part of the action within each industry through their most successful firms, hence facilitating the reallocation of the labor force and other factors of production and avoiding full deindustrialization within sectors.

There is an important qualitative difference between this process (and the limited resistance with which it is met) and the adjustment required if an entire industry (or the main production processes which it has traditionally sustained) is threatened with domestic extinction through a transfer of resources to new low-cost producers. In this so-called *inter-industry trade* the absorption of the work force which has become superfluous is more difficult than if certain production processes are simply being concentrated in fewer firms within a domestic industry. Trade with the new economies is often seen as dominated by inter-industry trade which accentuates adjustment problems. Hence it prompts much more easily demands from the sectors concerned and their employees that these problems be dealt with at the source—i.e., by impeding the rapid growth of trade—rather than corrected by subsequent redistributive measures.

As we shall see in the following chapters, the perceived difference in the two types of trade is greater than the available facts can sustain; an increasing share of trade with the new economies is beginning to look like the intra-industry trade among industrial countries. Furthermore, the new trading partners challenge not only industries in the OECD area which use unskilled labor relatively intensively, but also some industries which use either skilled labor or capital (or both) relatively intensively. This may take some of the perceived social inequity out of the challenge, but without modifying the perception that the industrial countries are faced with a threat to their industrial future which is qualitatively new and more ominous than anything experienced in the past. This perception is heightened by the awareness that new producers are often not subject to a number of the regulations with respect to the environment, labor conditions, workers rights, taxation, etc. which operate in broadly similar ways in most industrial countries—although the residual differences are sufficiently important to have prompted concerns in, e.g., some EU member states and in Canada over free trade with other industrial countries which maintain a laxer regime in these respects.

B. GROWING TENSIONS IN TRILATERAL LABOR MARKETS

Finally, and most important in recent years, the surge in trade with and foreign direct investment in new partners has coincided with growing tensions in labor markets in nearly all the Trilateral countries. These tensions manifest themselves in different ways in these countries, though in all of them employment in manufacturing has fallen, partly as a result of faster productivity increases in manufacturing and partly because of a shift in demand towards services. Figures I-2 and I-3 summarize the recent cumulative experience with respect to relative wage and employment trends for the lowest paid or less-skilled in a number of industrial countries.

In the *United States* the fall in manufacturing employment has been more than offset by job creation elsewhere in the economy, though typically at lower wages, hence giving rise to a category of "working poor." While real wages in the U.S. economy have been approximately stagnant for more than two decades, the lower-paid have experienced an absolute decline. This has heightened public sensitivity to trade developments which appear to threaten employment, whether they have arisen from the inclusion of a low-cost country (Mexico) in NAFTA or from globally freer trade.

In *Japan* the unemployment rate is still the lowest among the Trilateral countries, though higher than in the past, while there is no evidence of a widening of the differential between wages paid to skilled workers and the pay of the less-skilled. As discussed in more detail in the chapter on Japan, this seems to be due, in part at least, to pressures on the pay of white-collar employees (some of them indirectly related to globalization) which have prevented differentials over the less-skilled from widening. But the system of life-time employment has recently been called into question, as the large firms using the system appear to have used up the flexibility of reallocating their permanent labor force between activities.

In the *European Union*, a number of factors (of which the most important are minimum wages, the design of unemployment benefits and national wage bargaining systems with a pronounced element of solidarity towards the lower paid) have prevented wage differentials from widening—with the exception of the United Kingdom which has come to resemble the United States more than Continental Europe in its degree of flexibility in the structure of wages. Hence any tendency for the relative demand for less-skilled workers to weaken manifests itself in higher relative unemployment rather than in widening wage differentials (Figures I-2 and I-3).

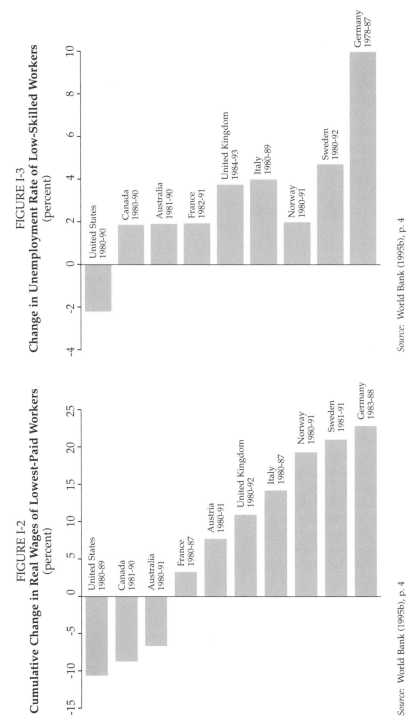

FIGURE I-2
Cumulative Change in Real Wages of Lowest-Paid Workers
(percent)

Source: World Bank (1995b), p. 4

FIGURE I-3
Change in Unemployment Rate of Low-Skilled Workers
(percent)

Source: World Bank (1995b), p. 4

Note: For Germany and Italy, this is the change in the unemployment rate for workers with less than a secondary education. For the other countries, it is the change in the unemployment rate of blue-collar workers.

C. THE LINKAGE BETWEEN GLOBALIZATION
AND GROWING LABOR MARKET TENSIONS

The main task of this report—which we take up in Chapters II-IV below—is to discuss the evidence of a link from the growth of trade with the non-OECD area (and foreign direct investment there by the industrial countries) to the growing tensions in Trilateral labor markets. As we have already argued, an important branch of trade theory relies on assumptions of competitive markets that lead directly to the conclusion that a link exists between the opening of trade and a relative decline in wages for the factor used relatively intensively in the production of imported goods, in this case unskilled labor. Other, less specific theories point to the same conclusion under conditions of initially imperfect competition, because trade flows erode privileged positions and the associated rents. The general public evidently tends to take the thrust of such analyses very literally, and it has found in the process of delocalization a wealth of anecdotal evidence which brings to life the vision of an inexorable process of job displacement in the direction of the low-cost producers. The very perception that a link exists could put the continuing evolution of trade and investment flows at risk.

Measuring the Linkage
Whether the link is primarily an interesting theoretical possibility or also a major element in explaining the unsatisfactory features of recent developments in Trilateral labor markets is, however, an empirical question. At first glance trade and investment flows with the new economies do not appear so far to have reached a size which could explain any major part of the deterioration over the recent past in relative wages and/or job opportunities of less-skilled workers in the Trilateral countries. Nor does it seem likely that even the more severe competitive pressures that are bound to arise in the future will lead to radically different conclusions, keeping in mind that even then the overwhelming part of the jobs in the Trilateral countries will be in the sectors serving the domestic economy on which globalization will have only a limited and indirect impact.

The main method which economists use to assess the link empirically is the so-called net factor content approach. This method calculates the input of unskilled labor into the output displaced by imported goods and into the additional exports to new trading partners, assuming balanced trade. Such calculations suggest that the net loss of unskilled jobs in the OECD countries is modest, and probably declining over time as trade flows take on an increasingly intra-industry nature. While this method is a useful first approximation, we discuss some reasons for thinking that it contains an optimistic bias due to its reliance on average factor inputs for industries rather than the input of unskilled labor in the parts of an industry most vulnerable to new, low-cost competition (i.e., firms likely to use above average inputs of unskilled labor). Data limitations unfortunately preclude a more systematic investigation of the size of this bias.

We limit our study of the linkage in various ways to make our study manageable. We focus on manufacturing, which is where the issue has primarily arisen, paying little attention to services. We concentrate on trade flows, since the problem has to show up there, paying less attention to foreign direct investment ("outsourcing") for which information is less readily available and comparable between countries. The evidence we can offer for Europe is necessarily less complete and systematic than for North America and Japan where the greater homogeneity of the Trilateral area and better data facilitate the analyses.

Furthermore, we do not look at the impact on the other side—the new exporters and/or host countries for foreign direct investment—although a careful study of factor inputs in non-OECD exports and shifts in the relative factor incomes in these countries would no doubt have yielded additional and potentially useful evidence in evaluating the new challenges with which the Trilateral countries are likely to be faced. Some of the non-OECD countries that have undertaken major economic reforms in recent years have experienced a sharp rise in income inequalities inside their own frontiers as some sectors or even regions begin to participate effectively in the international division of labor while the rest of the economy lags behind.

Alternative Explanations for the
Deteriorating Relative Position of the Less-Skilled
The most important limitation of our study may be, however, that we do not explore in any detail alternative explanations of why the relative position of the less-skilled part of the Trilateral countries' work force has deteriorated in the recent period, if, as we argue, increasing trade flows can not be held primarily or even significantly responsible for the observed deterioration. We do refer to the general

trend, observable in most Trilateral countries, for production techniques in manufacturing to move towards more intensive use of better-educated white-collar employees and away from less-skilled blue-collar workers. This bias in technological progress provides in our views the main explanation of the relative decline in the position of less-skilled workers. This leaves open, however, the interaction between this technological bias and globalization (in the sense used in this report) and in particular whether the latter (even though it is not in itself demonstrably a major explanatory factor) may have contributed more powerfully indirectly by accelerating the pace of technological change in manufacturing and by influencing its direction. We do not find this indirect linkage very plausible, since the present rate of technological change and its bias against the less-skilled parts of the workforce were established before globalization became a major phenomenon over the past decade.

Another explanatory factor advanced by some is immigration of less-skilled workers into Trilateral countries, increasing the supply of the less-skilled in the work force. We do not here treat labor migration in response to economic incentives and the special efforts in Trilateral countries to develop constructive immigration policies and to monitor illegal immigration. (Some of these issues were dealt with in an earlier report to the Trilateral Commission. See Meissner, Hormats, Garrigues Walker and Ogata [1993].)

**Small GDP Shares of Trade with
Non-OECD, Non-OPEC Countries**
Finally, we want to remind readers of the overwhelming size of the domestic economies in the three Trilateral regions relative to trade flows among them or with the non-OECD area. Furthermore, in absolute terms trade among the industrial countries remains more important than trade with new trading partners outside the Trilateral countries, even though trade flows between these two groups have grown considerably faster than intra-OECD trade. (For practical purposes it is useful to define these two groups as the OECD countries and the rest of the world, or non-OECD countries.) For each of the three Trilateral regions—North America, the European Union and Japan—exports and imports of goods each currently constitute between 6 and 9 per cent of total income or GDP—if one does not include the large trade flows inside North America and particularly inside the European Union (Tables I-1 and I-2). A similar geographical breakdown of trade in services is unfortunately not available.

TABLE I-1
Geographical Structure of OECD Exports
(% of GDP)

		1962	1972	1982	1992
United States		3.79	4.11	6.73	7.61
to	Europe	1.30	1.25	1.90	1.98
	North America	0.71	1.03	1.07	1.53
	Japan*	0.36	0.49	0.84	0.99
	OPEC	0.26	0.22	0.99	0.56
	Other Non-OECD	1.16	1.12	1.93	2.55
Europe		14.25	17.28	23.30	21.56
to	Europe	8.80	11.69	15.11	15.49
	North America	1.35	1.66	1.77	1.59
	Japan*	0.46	0.39	0.47	0.55
	OPEC	0.56	0.61	2.15	0.77
	Other Non-OECD	3.08	2.83	3.80	3.16
Japan		8.07	9.38	12.73	9.25
to	Europe	1.11	1.57	2.01	1.96
	North America	2.52	3.31	3.63	2.82
	OPEC	0.52	0.61	2.00	0.52
	Other Non-OECD	3.65	3.60	4.58	3.73

Source: OECD Jobs Study, Part I, p. 80
* including Australia and New Zealand

TABLE I-2
Geographical Structure of OECD Imports
(% of GDP)

	1962	1972	1982	1992
United States	2.86	4.60	7.74	9.03
from Europe	0.78	1.27	1.65	1.87
North America	0.64	1.23	1.47	1.68
Japan*	0.31	0.84	1.25	1.72
OPEC	0.19	0.23	0.73	0.37
Other Non-OECD	0.94	1.03	2.64	3.39
Europe	16.16	18.07	25.01	22.43
from Europe	8.93	11.71	15.07	15.47
North America	2.26	1.79	2.35	1.79
Japan*	0.57	0.63	0.93	1.14
OPEC	1.20	1.38	2.86	0.77
Other Non-OECD	3.20	2.56	3.80	3.26
Japan	9.24	7.70	11.77	6.33
from Europe	1.00	0.82	0.93	1.03
North America	3.39	2.30	2.63	1.64
Australia, NZ	0.77	0.81	0.72	0.38
OPEC	1.12	1.50	4.44	1.06
Other Non-OECD	2.96	2.27	3.05	2.22

Source: OECD Jobs Study, Part I, p. 79
* including Australia and New Zealand

Although trade in services has developed faster than trade in goods, these flows are still much smaller than trade in goods. As a first approximation one may conclude that, taken as regions, the three Trilateral regions show only a modest degree of openness to trade with each other and with the non-OECD area. Within the latter it is useful to distinguish between the oil-exporters and the rest of the non-OECD area, since trade with the oil exporters in both directions has been subject to violent gyrations following the two large jumps in energy prices in 1973-74 and 1979-80. Total trade in goods between each of the Trilateral areas and the still very heterogeneous rest of the non-OECD area currently amounts to somewhere between 2 and 4 per cent of regional GDP in each direction. These modest starting points should be kept in mind when discussing the future growth of trade. They provide a strong reminder that the "backlash against globalization"—as some observers have aptly labelled the current mood in many segments of public opinion in the Trilateral countries—is hard to justify on the basis of both past experience and the likely prospects for a continuing rapid rise in economic interaction with the non-OECD area.

*   *   *

Even against this background, some readers may find our report deficient since it does not enter into any detailed discussion as to how growing inequalities in wages or in job opportunities in the Trilateral countries should be addressed. We have regarded this subject—and, more broadly, the capacity of our societies to respond to the process of globalization and to the greater underlying challenge of technological developments in ways that constrain inequalities without harming the sources of long-run progress in living standards—as beyond the scope of the present report. We make no apologies for this lack of ambition since we have been asked to evaluate only the narrower problem of the impact of economic interaction with new trading partners. Having concluded that this interaction is a relatively minor factor in explaining the growing tensions in our labor markets (in the rather different form in which these tensions manifest themselves in the three Trilateral regions), we have not felt the analysis of remedies to improve the functioning of labor markets as a natural extension of our mandate.

II. THE UNITED STATES[1]

Importing from and investing in low-wage countries is by no means a new experience for the United States. Between 1950 and 1973, for example, America expanded its trade with the "low-wage" nations of Europe and Japan.[2] U.S. multinationals established extensive production facilities in Europe and licensed their technologies to foreigners. Yet over that period, not only were Europe and Japan able to grow rapidly and converge towards U.S. technology levels, but wages in the United States rose steadily and wage differentials between skilled and unskilled workers narrowed. Thus the American historical experience certainly shows that trade with low-wage countries is not incompatible with domestic prosperity in the high-wage nation.

But recent U.S. experience appears to be different. On the one hand, the United States economy has become increasingly open to foreign trade and investment over the past two decades. On the other, the United States has experienced little growth in real average compensation and wage inequality has increased dramatically.

The debate over the NAFTA in the early 1990s crystallized the fears about the effects of trade on U.S. wage performance. Ross Perot's allusion to the "giant sucking sound" of jobs moving southward resonated strongly with the anxieties of many Americans. Another concern in the NAFTA debate was over "runaway plants"—the relocation by multinationals to low-wage countries. Despite the passage of the NAFTA, these concerns remain highly salient in the

---

[1]This chapter concentrates on the United States. Card and Freeman (1994) compared labor market performance in Canada and the United States in the 1980s. "The two countries were buffeted by similar market forces...that made it difficult for less skilled workers throughout North America to prosper. Despite these shared conditions, and despite the great overall similarity of the American and Canadian economies, the two countries had different labor market and poverty outcomes....American policies generated substantial growth of low-wage jobs. Canadian policies generated nearly comparable employment growth while mitigating the forces that led to increased inequality and poverty in the United States. The experience of the 1980s shows vividly that even the relatively small differences in policies and institutions between Canada and the United States affected economic outcomes." (pp. 215, 217)

[2]In 1950, compensation in Germany and the United Kingdom was 13 and 17 percent of the average compensation level in the United States, respectively. In 1993, Mexican wages were about 12 percent of U.S. levels.

United States. In the 1996 Republican Presidential primaries, Patrick Buchanan garnered considerable support by proclaiming himself an "economic nationalist" and calling for the NAFTA's repeal, American withdrawal from the World Trade Organization and tariffs on imports from Japan, China and other low-wage countries.

Given the leadership role played by the United States in the world economy, the American debate cannot be ignored by the rest of the world. The U.S. experience is also particularly relevant for other reasons. U.S. wages are generally more flexible than those in other countries. If trade is having a major impact on the labor market, it might be expected to show up first in the American data. In addition, the United States has been more open to trade with developing countries than either Europe or Japan. As indicated in Figure II-1, compared with the European Community and Japan, the U.S. share of apparent consumption of manufactured goods imported from developing countries is higher and has risen more rapidly over the 1980s. And finally, the United States remains the world's largest multinational investor. American multinational firms span the globe; and if developments within these corporations affect domestic labor markets, the United States is the most susceptible.

This chapter therefore analyses the U.S. experience over the past two decades.[3] It deals with the two unfavorable features of U.S. wage performance separately. Section A considers the role of globalization in America's slow average wage growth over the past two decades. Section B considers the role of trade with developing countries in growing wage inequality over the same period. Section C then turns to the impact of international competition on high wage premiums. Section D examines the employment behavior of multinational corporations and Section E constructs a scenario to consider possible future effects of a large expansion of trade with developing countries.

The central conclusion of this analysis is that the role of globalization in poor U.S. labor market performance is much smaller than many believe. The slow rise in average U.S. compensation since 1979 reflects slow domestic productivity growth in sectors which are not subject to international competition. Growing wage inequality in the United States results primarily from changes in production methods and technologies. Trade with developing countries in particular appears to have played a relatively small role in the past and, surprisingly, even if imports from developing countries increase

---

[3]The chapter draws heavily on Lawrence (1996a).

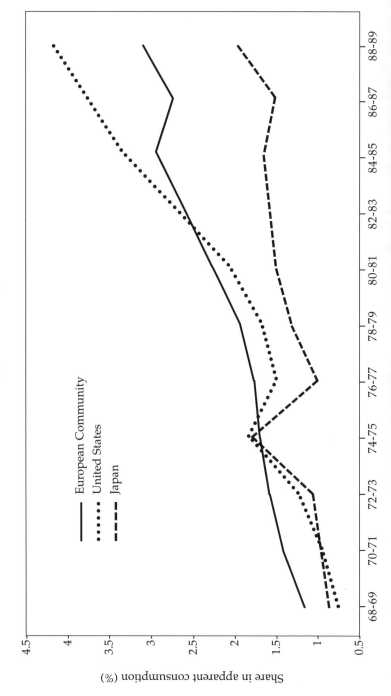

FIGURE II-1
Manufactured Imports from Developing Countries, 1968-89
(share in apparent consumption)

— European Community
······ United States
– – – Japan

rapidly in the future, the impact on wages of less-skilled workers is likely to be quite small. Nonetheless this trade could require considerable restructuring of the U.S. manufacturing sector.

A. WHY HAVE AVERAGE WAGES GROWN SO SLOWLY?

Between 1979 and 1995, real hourly compensation in the business sector of the United States increased by a total of just 5.4 percent—a pace of just 0.3 percent a year. This performance is a marked change for a country in which real wage growth averaged about two percent a year for over a century. Not unexpectedly, Americans have had great difficulty in accepting this new reality, and many have sought to blame others for their plight. Those fingered include the rich, particularly large multinational corporations that are said to have dramatically increased profits at the expense of their workers and relocated production facilities abroad; the poor, particularly welfare recipients who are seen as major beneficiaries of social programs which are excessively generous; international trade, with developing countries which compete on the basis of low wages, and with developed countries to whom America is seen to have ceded technological leadership; and immigrants, particularly those entering the United States illegally from Latin America. But the truth is that average American wages have grown slowly not because others have taken much bigger pieces of the worker's pie, but because the pie itself has expanded slowly. The major source of the slow growth in U.S. wages is not redistribution towards corporate profits, the rich, the poor or foreigners, but a decline in U.S. productivity growth, primarily in sectors of the U.S. economy not heavily involved in international trade, i.e. those outside manufacturing.

The simplest way to demonstrate this is to estimate what workers would have received had their share in U.S. income remained constant. To measure the total growth in the buying power of U.S. output, we take the value of the increased output produced in the U.S. business sector and deflate it by the U.S. consumer price index. As indicated in Table II-1, this measure indicates that between 1979 and 1995, the real income per hour produced by the U.S. business sector increased by 7.2 percent. If workers had received the same share of output in 1995 as they received in 1979, their compensation would have grown by 7.2 percent, in other words it would have been just 1.8 percent higher than it actually was. Qualitatively, therefore, the picture would have been essentially unchanged. Instead of

TABLE II-1
Real Compensation and Business Output

	1973	1979	1989	1994	1995
Business Output Per Hour (deflated by CPI) (1979=100)	96.4	100.0	103.9	106.6	107.2
Average Hourly Compensation (deflated by CPI) (1979=100)	95.8	100.0	102.3	104.5	105.4
Share of Compensation in Business Sector GDP (%)	65.1	66.2	64.3	64.5	64.4
Fixed Weight Terms of Trade (1979=100)	116.9	100.0	102.0	103.3	

Note: CPI = U.S. Consumer Price Index for all urban consumers

growing at 0.3 percent annually over the past fifteen years, real compensation would have grown at 0.4 percent annually.

In the recent economic expansion real hourly compensation has grown more slowly than real hourly incomes—a development which has received considerable press attention. But as reported in Table II-1, the share of compensation in 1995 was similar to that in 1989. This suggests the recent rebound in profits is essentially a cyclical rebound. Indeed between the cyclical peak in 1989 and 1995, both real hourly compensation and total income per hour in the corporate sector measured using the consumer price index increased by a total of 3 percent.[4]

Of course, real living standards in the United States depend not only on what American workers produce but also on their ability to exchange their output for foreign goods and services. If import prices rise more rapidly than U.S. domestic prices, the buying power of a given increase in domestic production will be lower. Johnson and

---

[4]The official measures of output per worker use the implicit price deflator for private corporate GDP. As analysed in Lawrence and Slaughter (1993), because this measure places a larger weight on investment goods, and does not reflect housing prices, it has risen more slowly than the consumer price index. This leads some to conclude erroneously that the slow rise in real compensation reflects redistribution towards profits.

Stafford (1993 January 5-7) have argued that America's loss of technological leadership has reduced the international buying power of U.S. workers. But in fact, over the past fifteen years the ratio of U.S. export to import prices—the terms of trade—have not moved adversely. As indicated in Table II-1, the fixed weight terms of trade have actually increased slightly.

In sum, the slump in real hourly compensation growth basically reflects a slump in domestic productivity growth. Although many studies of productivity focus on America's manufacturing performance, in fact, manufacturing productivity has grown at rates similar to that in the past. America's slow productivity growth has actually been concentrated in sectors of the economy that are almost totally sheltered from international competition such as construction, electricity, real estate and most importantly in services.[5]

B. THE SMALL ROLE IN GROWING WAGE INEQUALITY OF DEVELOPING COUNTRY TRADE

While the soaring salaries of corporate executives grab U.S. headlines, the most quantitatively important shift in the U.S. earnings distribution has occurred within labor compensation between educated and less-well-educated workers. Between 1978 and 1990, as estimated by Lawrence (1996a) for example, the wages of full-time manufacturing workers with some college education increased by fifteen percent more than those with a high-school education or less. Similarly, as shown in Figure II-2, the ratio of compensation of (non-sales) white-collar workers to blue-collar workers increased by 12 percent between 1980 and 1991, although since that time the ratio has remained fairly constant. As Figure II-2 also indicates, real compensation of white-collar workers rose by 17 percent, while real blue-collar worker compensation increased by just 5 percent.

The relative increase in the wages of educated workers and managers in the 1980s occurred despite the fact that the share of educated workers in the labor force rose rapidly. Similarly, relative female wages rose despite the relatively rapid increase in female participation.[6] To explain the growing wage dispersion, therefore, most analysts have turned to demand-side explanations such as trade and technology.

---

[5]For a more complete discussion, see Lawrence (1996b).
[6]Supply side stories which emphasize differences in growth rates may do better. While the relative supply of educated labor increased in the 1980s, it grew more slowly than in the 1970s. Thus in the face of a given increase in the relative demand for skilled labor, wages of skilled workers would rise. For an argument along these lines, see Katz and Murphy (1992).

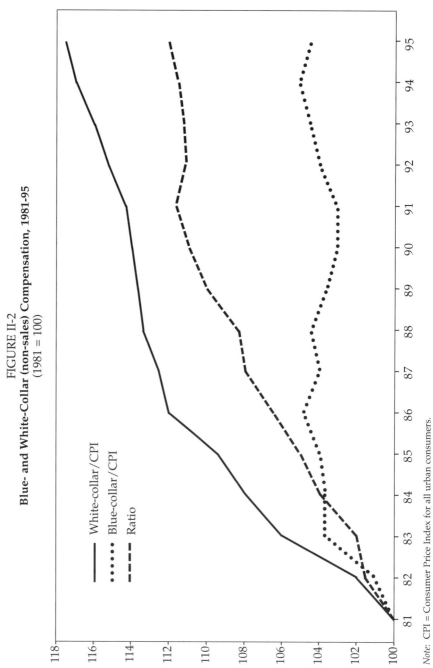

FIGURE II-2
Blue- and White-Collar (non-sales) Compensation, 1981-95
(1981 = 100)

Note: CPI = Consumer Price Index for all urban consumers.

Quantitative Evidence

The empirical evidence in support of trade as an explanation remains a matter of contention. Several researchers have found correlations between the emergence of trade deficits and rising wage inequality. But studies which have gauged the quantitative impact of trade by using trade volume measures obtain relatively small effects. One such methodology is the net factor content approach which treats imports as increasing the supply of productive factors and exports as increasing the demand. Borjas, Freeman and Katz (1991) estimated the quantities of educated and uneducated labor embodied in U.S. manufactured exports and imports. Since U.S. imports contain relatively more uneducated labor, an increase in net imports raises the relative supply of uneducated labor and drives down its relative wage. Their quantitative estimates, however, suggest the impact has been relatively small. They conclude that trade flows explained at most 15 percent (i.e., 1.9 percentage points) of the 12.4 percent increase between 1980 and 1988 in the earnings differential between college-educated workers and their high-school-educated counterparts. Similarly, Jeffrey Sachs and Howard Shatz (1994) construct a counterfactual scenario in which U.S. net trade balances remain a constant share of domestic spending between 1978 and 1990. They then compare this to the actual outcome in 1990 and conclude that trade reduced U.S. manufacturing employment by 5.9 percent between 1978 and 1990—a number equal to about one percent of total U.S. employment. Sachs and Shatz also conclude that manufactured trade with developing countries reduced overall U.S. manufacturing employment by 4.8 percent, and production and non-production manufacturing employment by 5.1 and 3.9 percent respectively. Taking account of the fact that production workers in manufacturing accounted for only about a quarter of manufacturing workers in the U.S. economy as a whole, the impact of these effects on the overall relative demand for such workers was small.

When one considers with whom America trades and the scale of U.S. trade, it is not surprising that estimates of the factor supplies embodied in U.S. manufacturing trade indicate relatively small effects on wages—particularly for trade with developing countries. In 1990, 70 percent of America's manufacturing imports came from OECD countries—countries with endowments and wage levels very similar to America's.[7] U.S. imports from developing countries did increase

---

[7] In 1980, hourly compensation in other OECD countries was 83 percent of U.S. levels; this dropped to 64 percent by 1985 but then increased to 103 percent by 1990.

rapidly over the decade but from a low base. In 1990 for example, imports of manufactured goods (classified on an international trade basis) amounted to $115.8 billion or 2.1 percent of U.S. GNP, versus 1.2 percent in 1981. A change of this magnitude—less than one percent of GNP—is unlikely to have an overwhelming impact on the overall labor market.

Between 1978 and 1990, the U.S. trade balance in manufactured goods with developing countries shifted from a surplus of $32.8 billion to a deficit of $34.9 billion. In 1978, the surplus with developing countries in manufactured goods was equal to 5 percent of overall value-added in U.S. manufacturing; in 1990 the deficit was equal to 2.6 percent. Overall, therefore the shift was equal to 7.6 percent of value-added in manufacturing which is in turn less than twenty percent of U.S. GDP. Moreover, since manufactured products embody primary commodities and services not produced in manufacturing, this ratio exaggerates the negative effect of the manufacturing trade deficit on manufacturing value-added and employment.[8]

Price Evidence

Some economists have been critical of these approaches looking at trade quantities. In particular, Bhagwati (1994) and Leamer (1996) emphasize that trade volumes might not be good indicators of trade pressures. Indeed, one can think of examples in which just the threat of increased imports could drive domestic wages down without leading to increased trade flows. These economists regard price evidence as more significant. They emphasize that if trade lowered the relative wages of unskilled workers, we would also expect to see a decline in the relative prices of goods which are produced using unskilled labor relatively intensively. As large, labor-intensive economies lower their trade barriers and enter the world market their presence would first be felt through an increase in the global relative supply of unskilled-labor-intensive products. This, in turn, would lower the relative price of these products on world markets thereby putting downward pressure on the wages of unskilled workers in the developed world.

Several studies of the price evidence have been made. While some

---

[8]While small in the aggregate, it should be noted that the impact of trade is not insubstantial for particular sectors. In particular, imports from developing countries are concentrated in a few major industries. Apparel (15 percent), electrical goods (18.4), so-called non-electrical machinery which includes computers (10.4), miscellaneous manufacturing (8 percent), and leather (6.2) account for well over half of all imports. In some of these sectors, the effects on overall value-added were important.

studies do report declines in the relative price of unskilled-labor-intensive goods in the '70s and '90s, most do not find such declines over the 1980s, the period in which most of the wage inequality emerged.[9] Paul Krugman (1995b) has noted that under some circumstances the conflict between price and quantity evidence need not arise. Indeed, he shows how shifts in trade quantities can provide a clue about the changes in prices in the face of an increase in labor-intensive imports from developing countries (see also Krugman [1995a]). Applying this approach Krugman concludes that only small relative changes in the prices of labor-intensive goods took place over the 1980s, and these had small effects—on the order of less than three percent—on the relative wages of unskilled U.S. workers.

In sum, both the quantitative and price evidence suggest small or negligible effects of developing country trade on growing U.S. wage inequality. This has led most economists to assign a major role in this inequality to technology (Bound and Johnson 1992). Firms have increasingly substituted educated workers for less-educated workers. While the precise roles of increased use of computers and other shifts in labor-management relations in this shift are difficult to determine, in general changes in methods of production appear to be the most important source of America's increased wage inequality.

C. WAGE PREMIUMS OF UNSKILLED WORKERS IN CONCENTRATED IMPORT-COMPETING INDUSTRIES

The empirical work just surveyed assumes that labor markets are highly competitive, with workers receiving similar wages based on their skill levels, regardless of where they work. This overlooks the possibility that trade and the possibilities of overseas investment reduce wages of the unskilled by weakening the bargaining power of trade unions and by lowering the returns to industry-specific human capital and other determinants of industry-specific wage premiums. Indeed Borjas and Ramey (1993) argue that international competition has forced down relative wages in highly concentrated import-competing industries and caused the loss of jobs in sectors which provide high-wages for workers with low skills. As shown in Tables

---

[9]Lawrence and Slaughter (1993) found that over the 1980s, the relative import and export prices of unskilled-labor-intensive goods actually increased slightly. Sachs and Shatz (1994) challenged these findings as unduly influenced by computer prices. When they drop computers they obtain a negative but small and statistically insignificant relationship between price changes and skill intensity. Leamer (1995) confirms that in the 1980s relative prices of labor-intensive products did not fall, although he does find declines in the 1970s. Cooper (1994) finds that relative clothing and footwear prices did not decline in the 1980s. Krueger (1995) finds evidence over the period 1989-95 of relative price declines in unskill-intensive products.

II-2A and II-2B, however, contrary to the arguments of Borjas and Ramey, the relative wages of unskilled workers in concentrated manufacturing industries have not fallen by substantial amounts. Nor have union wage increases lagged behind those in the rest of the economy. Between 1979 and 1990 relative wages in the concentrated import-competing sectors pointed to by Borjas and Ramey declined by just two percent. With the notable exception of primary metals, no decline is apparent in relative earnings in major high-rent sectors. Hence this channel does not appear to explain much of the overall shift in the wage distribution.

In addition, Lawrence (1996a) estimates the impact of trade on the availability of high-wage jobs for unskilled workers. He finds that trade cannot account for more than a trivial proportion of the wage differential between workers with only a high school education and those with a college education. At most the effect appears to be on the order of 0.2 or 0.3 percent.[10] A similar conclusion is reached from considering the effects of declining employment opportunities in U.S. manufacturing due both to trade and other sources of change. Between 1978 and 1990, the share of employment in manufacturing declined from 24 to 18 percent. If unskilled workers receive premiums as high as 20 percent in manufacturing and 6 percent (24-18) of unskilled workers lost this premium between 1978 and 1990, this translates into a decline in average wages of all unskilled workers of just 1.2 percent.

In sum, while international competition has undoubtedly put some downward pressure on wages in a few sectors, the impact is not sufficiently large to explain much of the pervasive shifts in wage inequality that emerged in the 1980s.

D. MULTINATIONALS AND OUTSOURCING

Corporate downsizing has received considerable attention in the United States. As reported in Table II-3, U.S. firms with foreign operations have not contributed to employment growth within the United States over the 1980s—a remarkable result given the rise of about 30 percent in overall U.S. employment in that period. Moreover, between 1989 and 1993 employment in U.S. multinational parent operations declined by 6 percent, while employment in the economy as a whole increased by 2 percent.

---

[10]Ravenga (1992) found some evidence of downward relative wage pressure due to imports but the effects were not large.

TABLE II-2A
Changes in Earnings:
Concentrated Manufacturing Industries
Compared to All Manufacturing Industries

	1979	1990	'90/'79
High-School-Educated (Unskilled) Employment			
Concentrated Manufacturing Industries	303.10	476.37	1.57
All Manufacturing Industries	251.45	403.25	1.60
Concentrated/All	1.21	1.18	
Employment Share of Concentrated in All	0.20	0.18	
College-Educated Employment			
Concentrated Manufacturing Industries	397.48	731.08	1.84
All Manufacturing Industries	361.43	667.16	1.85
Concentrated/All	1.10	1.10	
Employment Share of Concentrated in All	0.25	0.24	

Source: CPS Tapes

TABLE II-2B
Changes in Earnings:
Union Workers Compared to Non-Union Workers
(1989=100)

	1979	1989	1995
Union Workers	60.4	100	122.7
Non-Union Workers	60.9	100	123.3
Union/Non-Union	99.2	100	99.1

Source: Employment Cost Index

TABLE II-3
Employment in U.S. Multinational Corporations
(thousands)

	1977	1989	1993	% change '89/'77	% change '93/'89
Employment in U.S. Parents					
All industries	18,885	18,785	17,682	-1	-6
Manufacturing	11,775	10,127	9,246	-14	-9
Employment in Foreign Affiliates					
All industries	7,196.7	6,622.1	6,731.1	-8	+2
of which:					
Canada	1,064	955.2	874.9	-10	-8
Europe	3,110	2,699.1	2,733.1	-13	+1
Japan	389	392.2	411.3	+1	+5
Developing Countries	2,175	2,121.1	2,259.8	-2	+7
of which:					
Mexico	370.1	527.2	666.1	+42	+26
All Others	1,804.9	1,593.9	1,593.7	-12	0
Manufacturing	4,849	4,191	4,019	-14	-4
of which:					
Canada	614.8	476.6	406.9	-23	-14
Europe	2,348.4	1,783.4	1,652.8	-24	-7
Japan	185.5	240.3	232.7	+30	-3
Developing Countries	1,533.4	1,570.9	1,618.6	+2	+3
of which:					
Mexico	302.8	443.5	490.5	+46	+11
All Others	1,230.6	1,127.4	1,128.1	-8	0

Sources: US Direct Investment Abroad: 1977 Benchmark Survey; US Direct Investment Abroad: 1989 Benchmark Survey; Survey of Current Business, June 1995

Note: All data refer to non-bank parents and affiliates, both majority-owned and minority-owned.

Multinational firms are particularly important in the U.S. manufacturing sector—indeed they account for about half of all manufacturing employment. However, between 1977 and 1989, U.S. employment in manufacturing multinationals fell 14 percent (from 11.78 to 10.13 million)—considerably faster than the drop of 1.2 percent in overall manufacturing employment over the same period. Similarly between 1989 and 1993, employment in multinational parents fell by almost 9 percent compared with a 7.2 percent drop in U.S. manufacturing employment as a whole.

The sluggish employment growth in U.S. multinationals has been attributed by many Americans to the impact of their foreign operations. It is widely perceived in the United States that many jobs formerly in these firms have moved abroad. Drawn by low labor costs and low labor standards, MNCs are seen as having relocated their production towards low-wage countries. In particular, the jobs of blue-collar workers are viewed as vulnerable to this development. Such international outsourcing could, in principle, provide an alternative explanation of the widespread decline in both relative blue-collar wages and in the ratio of blue to white-collar workers employed in U.S. manufacturing.

However, changes in the data between 1977 and 1989 reported in Table II-3 do not support the common perception that overseas employment in U.S.-owned foreign affiliates has increased. Indeed, between 1977 and 1989, employment in the foreign affiliates of U.S. MNCs declined at a faster rate (8 percent) than in their parent operations. The 14 percent decline in employment in foreign manufacturing affiliates matched that of their U.S. parents. This decline in foreign-based U.S.-owned manufacturing was mainly due to shrinkage in the European and Canadian operations of U.S. MNCs where total employment fell by 24 percent and 23 percent respectively.

There has been a rise in employment in foreign affiliates in developing countries both in manufacturing and since 1989 in all industries but the increase has not been large or widespread. Indeed, it is more than accounted for by the rise in employment in foreign affiliates located in Mexico. There is no evidence of a mass migration by U.S. firms to increase employment in their foreign low-wage affiliates. Outside Mexico, between 1977 and 1993, employment in manufacturing foreign affiliates in developing countries has actually fallen by 8 percent. Including Mexico, employment increased from 1.53 to 1.62 million, a rise of just 109,000 jobs—the equivalent of about half a percent of U.S. employment in manufacturing.

Data on production worker employment is available for majority-owned foreign affiliates in developing countries in 1977 and 1989. Of the 60,000 growth recorded in employment in these affiliates, only 4,000 occurred in the employment of production workers. There is, therefore, little evidence that on balance large numbers of production worker jobs are shifting within U.S. multinationals away from the United States towards the developing countries.

It is also noteworthy that the ratio of production to non-production workers employed in U.S. manufacturing operations worldwide has fallen precipitously. Indeed the declines are of similar magnitude in U.S. manufacturing parents (-15.7 percent) and in their affiliates in developing countries (-13.6 percent). If U.S. multinationals were primarily driven to seek low-wage workers abroad, we might expect to see the ratio of production to non-production workers falling in the United States and rising abroad. Instead, this ratio moves in the same direction both at home and abroad. Together the picture that emerges appears to be far more consistent with the notion of a common shift in technology rather than of expanding trade. Worldwide, we see a rise in the relative employment of non-production workers despite the increase in their relative wage.

Outsourcing

As might be expected for a period in which the U.S. trade deficit increased, between 1982 and 1989 there was a rapid increase in the purchases of manufactured goods by U.S.-based MNCs from their foreign affiliates. These purchases increased from $25 billion in 1982 to $61.2 billion in 1989. Purchases from unaffiliated foreigners increased even more rapidly from $16.1 to $45.3 billion. While the increase has been rapid, these imports still represent only a small share of the total sales of U.S. MNC parents, rising from 4.1 percent in 1982 to 6.8 percent in 1989. Moreover, these numbers refer to purchases from both developed and developing countries. Manufactured imports from developing countries were roughly a third of these shares. These effects are thus simply too small to have employment and wage shift effects of the size they are alleged to have.[11]

---

[11]The Bureau of Economic Analysis (BEA) of the U.S. Commerce Department reaches similar conclusions. In the *Survey of Current Business* (July 1993) they compared employment patterns in high- and low-wage countries over the period 1982-91. The low-wage share of employment in majority-owned foreign affiliates (MOFA) increased by 3 percentage points to 34 percent. Between '82 and '89 they find that the domestic content of U.S. parents' output in manufacturing decreased from 96 to 93 percent.

E. THE FUTURE

Almost all the recent studies of the links between trade and wages have looked backwards, considering the impact of trade on the labor market over the 1980s. But the relationship between trade and wages could become more relevant in the coming decades.[12] In what follows, I will present evidence which suggests that while growing international trade between the United States and developing countries could lead to lower relative and real wages for unskilled workers, the fears of large absolute and relative wage losses for less-skilled workers appear misplaced. If sustained over the next fifteen years, an expansion in trade between the United States and the developing countries at the double-digit pace of the past decade would bring about a major change the structure of U.S. manufacturing production. In particular, the United States could see a decline in large segments of its basic industrial activities as these are replaced by imports from emerging markets. However, matching this decline will be an expansion of skill-intensive activities that will provide an offsetting source of growth. While trade could effect major shifts in the structure of U.S. production, its impact on the wage structure is unlikely to be large.[13] The basic reason for this small impact is that manufacturing in general, and those sectors potentially vulnerable to developing country competition in particular, comprise a relatively small share of total employment.

In what follows, we explore the implications of a very large expansion in U.S. manufactured goods trade using data on the U.S. economy in 1990. *We obtain an upper-bound impact on the U.S. labor market by assuming that industries which compete with manufactured imports from developing countries are totally eliminated. The United States shifts into non-competing industries, and workers find jobs in sectors producing exports or non-traded goods and services.*

High-Skill and Basic Industries

Which industries are potentially most vulnerable to competition from developing countries? Table II-4 lists U.S. industries ranked according to the share of full-time workers with a high-school education or less—"high-school workers"—in the labor force in 1990.[14] The industries range from Tobacco, in which high school workers

---

[12]See Slaughter (1994).

[13]This analysis draws heavily on Lawrence (1996a) in which a more extensive and rigorous discussion of the scenario is provided.

[14]Industry SIC 29, petroleum refining, has been excluded.

TABLE II-4
U.S. Manufacturing Industries:
Trade and Employment Characteristics, 1990

SIC		hs /emp	ldc exp /va	ldc imp /va	share of ldc exp	share of ldc imp	share of man emp	share of man va	hs/col wages	hs/col earnings
21.00	Tobacco	0.43	0.06	0.00	0.01	0.00	0.00	0.02	0.70	0.35
38.00	Instruments	0.45	0.10	0.06	0.05	0.02	0.04	0.04	0.56	0.31
28.00	Chemicals	0.46	0.10	0.02	0.14	0.02	0.07	0.12	0.62	0.35
27.00	Printing	0.49	0.00	0.01	0.00	0.00	0.08	0.08	0.73	0.42
35.00	Non-Elec Machinery	0.50	0.16	0.12	0.19	0.11	0.12	0.10	0.64	0.39
36.00	Electrical Machinery	0.50	0.14	0.20	0.18	0.20	0.10	0.11	0.55	0.35
37.00	Transportation Equipment	0.53	0.13	0.06	0.17	0.06	0.13	0.11	0.67	0.43
	Total High-Skill	**0.50**	**0.11**	**0.08**	**0.74**	**0.42**	**0.54**	**0.57**	**0.63**	**0.39**
26.00	Paper Products	0.65	0.06	0.02	0.03	0.01	0.04	0.05	0.67	0.55
39.00	Miscellaneous Manufact	0.67	0.07	0.60	0.01	0.09	0.02	0.02	0.62	0.55
30.00	Rubber	0.67	0.04	0.09	0.02	0.03	0.04	0.04	0.67	0.58
32.00	Stone, Clay & Glass	0.68	0.03	0.06	0.01	0.02	0.03	0.03	0.64	0.58
34.00	Metal Products	0.69	0.05	0.05	0.03	0.03	0.06	0.06	0.67	0.59
20.00	Food	0.71	0.05	0.05	0.06	0.05	0.09	0.11	0.66	0.62
33.00	Primary Metals	0.73	0.08	0.16	0.04	0.06	0.04	0.04	0.72	0.87
25.00	Furniture	0.80	0.02	0.12	0.00	0.02	0.03	0.02	0.69	0.73
24.00	Lumber	0.81	0.05	0.06	0.01	0.01	0.03	0.02	0.67	0.74
31.00	Leather	0.81	0.15	2.01	0.01	0.07	0.01	0.00	0.57	0.71
22.00	Textiles	0.82	0.06	0.16	0.01	0.03	0.03	0.02	0.64	0.74
23.00	Apparel	0.85	0.05	0.68	0.02	0.16	0.05	0.03	0.54	0.75
	Total Basic	**0.73**	**0.05**	**0.15**	**0.26**	**0.58**	**0.46**	**0.43**	**0.63**	**0.64**

Notes: hs/emp = share of full-time employment with high school degree or less; ldc exp = U.S. exports of manufactured goods to developing countries; ldc imp = U.S. imports of manufactured goods from developing countries; man emp = employment in manufacturing; man va = value added in manufacturing

accounted for just 43 percent of employment, to Apparel in which they constituted 85 percent. The industries seem to fall into two distinct groups. There is one group of seven industries in which high-school employment shares range from 43 to 53 percent and a second group with shares ranging between 65 and 85 percent. There are no two-digit industries between 53 and 65 percent. This suggests a natural division. The first group we define as "high-skill" industries. It includes printing and tobacco plus the industries that are usually classified as "high-tech," namely chemicals, machinery and instruments. The second group, which we define as "basic," includes all other manufacturing industries.

Clearly, given the level of aggregation, this is a fairly crude approximation, but it does have quite strong predictive value with respect to trade with developing countries. The high-skill industries accounted for about three-quarters of all U.S. manufactured exports to developing countries, while the basic industries accounted for almost sixty percent of U.S. manufactured imports from developing countries. Moreover, exports to developing countries count for much higher shares of value added in the high-skill industries (11 percent) than in the basic industries (5 percent). On the other hand, the ratio of manufactured imports to domestic value-added is much higher for low-skill (15 percent) than for high-skill industries (8 percent).

An Extreme Scenario

This classification of U.S. industries suggests an extreme scenario in which the United States becomes fully specialized in high-skill products. In this scenario, as set out in Table II-5, the United States completely replaces the 1990 domestic value-added of $552 billion produced in basic industries with imports from developing countries. In turn, exports (and production) of the high-skill industries expand by an additional $552 billion in proportion to their 1990 output shares. This is a very dramatic scenario. In 1990, U.S. imports from developing countries of manufactured goods amounted to $140 billion. In the alternative scenario they are assumed to increase by $550 billion to $690 billion—in other words, there is a five-fold increase. If this increase took place over a fifteen-year period it would correspond to an annual growth rate of 11.3 percent. These effects would build up over time and become larger in later years when trade volumes are larger. After ten years, only about half of the effects would be felt.

As reported in Table II-5, given constant ratios of inputs to outputs, this switch eliminates the demand for the 8.7 million workers

Globalization and Trilateral Labor Markets

TABLE II-5
Future Scenario: United States

		High-Skill Mnfctrg	Basic Mnfctrg	All Mnfctrg	Non- Mnfctrg	U.S. Ecnmy
1990 Actual						
(1)	Value Added ($billions)	742.05	552.45	1294.50		
(2)	Employment (millions)	10.18	8.68	18.86	86.17	105.03
(3)	ValueAdded/Emp (1)/(2)	72.89	63.65	68.64		
(4)	High School Emp (millions)	5.08	6.36	11.44	39.85	51.29
(5)	College Emp (millions)	5.10	2.32	7.42	46.32	53.74
(6)	HS/Emp (4)/(2)	0.50	0.73	0.61	0.46	0.49
(7)	HS/COL (4)/(5)	1.00	2.74	1.54	0.86	0.954
Hypothetical						
(8)	Value Added	1284.50	0.00	1294.50		
(9)	Employment (8)/(3)	17.76	0.00	17.76		
(10)	High School Emp (6)*(9)	8.86	0.00	8.86	39.85	48.71
(11)	College Emp (9)-(10)	8.90	0.00	8.90	46.32	55.22
(12)	HS/COL (10)/(11)	1.00		1.00	0.86	0.882
Hypothetical - Actual						
(13)	Employment (9)-(2)	+7.58	-8.68	-1.10		
(14)	High School Emp (10)-(4)	+3.78	-6.36	-2.58	0.00	-2.58
(15)	College Emp (11)-(5)	+3.80	-2.32	+1.48	0.00	1.48
(16)	HS/COL (12)-(7)	0.00		-0.55		-0.072
(17)	HS/COL as % of Actual (7)					-7.5%

employed in basic industries (6.4 million high-school workers and 2.3 million college workers). On the other hand, the increase in value-added of the high-skill manufacturing sector by $552 billion adds demand for 7.6 million workers, split evenly between high-school and college workers. All told therefore, this substitution results in an excess supply of 2.6 million high-school workers and an excess demand for 1.5 million college workers. Given this alternative production structure for manufacturing, with no change in relative wages, the demanded economy-wide employment ratio of high-school to college workers is 88.2 percent. In fact, in 1990, the ratio was 95.4 percent. *Thus as compared to 1990, the relative demand for high school workers would decline by 7.5 percent.* To clear the labor market, therefore, the relative wage of high-school workers would have to fall to encourage firms in both high-skill manufacturing and the non-manufacturing economy to hire more high-school and fewer college workers.

A key question, therefore, is the sensitivity of the relative demand for different types of workers to relative wages. Although the empirical literature provides a wide range of estimates,[15] it is reasonable to assume that for each fall of one percent in the relative wages of unskilled workers, relative demand increases by one percent. This assumption is also convenient, since it implies that to increase the relative demand for high-school workers by 7.5 percent requires a proportional decline in the *relative* high-school wage, i.e. of 7.5 percent.[16]

Observations

Why is there a limit on the extent to which the relative wages of unskilled U.S. workers fall? Indeed, there is a theorem in international trade theory known as factor price equalization which leads some to conclude that free trade with developing countries will drive the wages of unskilled U.S. workers down to Chinese or Indian levels. But the theorem only holds under conditions of incomplete specialization. Once countries become fully specialized, the strong links between international wages and product prices break down. For example, if a country has no domestic production of clothing, imports of clothing will no longer directly affect wages. One way for firms in developed economies to avoid head-to-head competition with developing countries, therefore, is to specialize in producing products which developing countries do not produce. Under these conditions, wages and other factor prices in the developed countries will be determined only by the goods and services that they actually produce: namely, those that are exported and those that are not-

---

[15]For a survey see Hamermesh (1986).
[16]Deardorff and Staiger (1988) show that if product expenditures and factor shares remain constant shares of income, the change in relative wages will be proportional to the changes in total relative factor supplies represented by changes in the net factor content of trade.

traded. Put more simply, the floor on the wages of unskilled workers in the developed countries is not what workers earn in the textile industries of China and India but what they can earn if they are all employed in export and domestic industries.

Qualifications

While useful as a first effort, several questions can legitimately be raised about this scenario:

Growth. First, by using data from 1990 we ignored the fact that over a fifteen-year period, there will be productivity improvements and the economy is likely to grow. Indeed, over a fifteen-year period, with output per worker in manufacturing increasing at the 2.5 percent annual rate it averaged between 1979 and 1994, for example, the employment impact of these shifts would be reduced by 44 percent. Taking productivity growth into account, therefore, suggests that an 11.3 percent annual growth rate over fifteen years in imports from developing countries would reduce the relative demand for high school workers by $0.56 * 7.5 = 4.1$ percent. This is therefore a more realistic estimate of the displacement effects of the volume effects in the scenario.

Labor Force Growth. Second, the U.S. labor force is likely to grow over this period at an annual rate of around one percent. This implies that the employment shifts represented by these trade flows will represent relatively smaller shares of the labor force. Assuming a proportional increase in the ratio of high-school to college workers, this would reduce the estimates of relative wage changes by an additional fifteen percent, i.e to $.85 * 4.1 = 3.5$ percent.

Induced Demand and Supply Changes. Third, we have taken the relative supplies and demands for these factors as given. But there are likely to be responses in both demand and supply which will reduce this effect. On the demand side, technological innovation could occur which saves on the use of college workers and makes more intensive use of high-school workers. On the supply side, the lower relative wage of high-school workers implies an increase in the return to education. If it induces workers and new labor force entrants to invest more in education, this will reduce the relative supply of high-school workers and bolster their relative wages. The net result would therefore be a shift that is smaller than 4.1 percent over fifteen years.

Product Price and Real Wage Changes. Thus far the analysis has estimated the impact of trade on relative wages. We know from trade theory, however, that in this scenario the real wage of skilled workers will rise and the real wage of unskilled workers will fall. To obtain explicit relative price and real wage effects associated with this scenario, Lawrence and Evans (1996) simulate the scenario with a general equilibrium, two-factor, three-sector model calibrated on 1990 U.S. data.[17] The shift in resources in the scenario leads to an increase in the relative price of high-skill (and non-traded) goods of only about 2 percent. The real wages of skilled workers rise by 3.3 percent, while the real wages of unskilled workers fall by 4.4 percent.

In sum, as we would expect from trade theory, unskilled workers are hurt by trade. If this scenario took place over a fifteen-year period and given an increase in productivity and growth in the labor force, the decline in real wages would be about 2.5 percent instead of 4.4 percent. Since this impact would be felt over fifteen years, if average real wages in the United States were to rise by one percent per year due to higher domestic productivity, workers could absorb the change due to trade and still experience real earnings growth of 0.84 percent annually.

Rents. The simulations have assumed that average wages earned by high-school and college workers are the same throughout the economy. But in fact, there are differences. Katz and Summers (1989) have estimated the wage premiums for two-digit manufacturing for managers and laborers. Ascribing their estimates of rents for managers to college workers and for laborers to high-school workers suggests that on average the rents of managers and workers in basic industries are 6 and 2 percent respectively, while for college and high-school workers in high-skill industries on average they are 15 and 13 percent. Thus, given these rents, the shift in employment from the basic to the high-skill sector would increase average rents for both types of workers. This would be the source of additional gains from trade.[18] On average, for employment shifts laid out in the net factor content scenario described above, average economy-wide rents earned by high-school and college workers would rise by 0.7 and 0.8 of one percent respectively. Taking these into account therefore leaves

---

[17]The model has a non-traded goods sector which accounts for 82.5 percent of consumption and high-skill and basic manufacturing industries which account for 10 and 7.5 percent respectively. It has Cobb-Douglas production and consumption functions and is parameterized using the data in Table 6.1.

[18]Indeed, Katz and Summers (1989) find that U.S. export industries provide higher wage premiums than those competing with imports.

[19]See World Bank (1995), chapter 3.

the impact of trade on relative wages unchanged, but implies a decline of (2.5 - 0.8) just 1.7 percent in real wages of unskilled workers in the face of a fivefold increase in import volumes.

Services Trade. Finally, there is the issue of non-manufactured goods trade. There are several areas in which improvements in communications have increased the scope of what may be traded. In particular, as an example in the low-skill area, data-processing activities once performed domestically in OECD countries are increasingly undertaken abroad. On the other hand, even high-skill firms are finding it feasible to use software and other talented engineers in developing countries. Nonetheless, if the experience in goods trade is indicative, it remains likely that services trade between OECD and developing countries will occur mainly along skill lines, with the OECD exporting skill-intensive services and importing unskilled-intensive services. The literature on the potential for providing long-distance services has been surveyed by the World Bank (1995a).[19] They report studies showing that an estimated 12 to 16 percent of employment in services in the G-7 countries is in services that could, technically, be provided at long distance. However, there are many activities that for strategic reasons (such as preserving proprietary information) companies are reluctant to outsource, particularly internationally. The Bank therefore estimates that between 1 and 5 percent of the total employment in services in the G-7 economies are contestable internationally. This suggests a potential market for such exports in the United States in 1990 dollars of between $14.4 and $43.1 billion, and in the G-7 of between $40.3 and $121 billion. While the high estimate of $43.1 billion represents about thirty percent of the value of U.S. manufactured imports in 1990, if the internationally contestable share remained a similar proportion of employment over the next fifteen years, it would be too small to have a major impact on the calculations in this scenario. Apparently, therefore, the overwhelming majority of output outside of manufacturing will remain non-traded.

In summary, this exercise suggests that over a fifteen-year period, rapid increases in U.S. trade with developing countries could depress the relative and absolute wages of unskilled U.S. workers. In its most stark form, once productivity growth is taken into account, the effects are on the order of about a two-and-a-half percent decline in real wages over a fifteen-year period, and an effect that is even smaller once the impact of wages premiums in the export sector is accounted for. In an economy in which average real wage growth was fairly strong, this type of change, of about a sixth of a percent a year, would not be a major issue—particularly if there were other positive effects on the less-skilled because of other changes in the labor market. However, if combined with continued strength in skill-biased technological change, dealing with unskilled workers will present an important challenge for policy.

It should be emphasized, moreover, that this is an upper-bound impact. It ignores the fact that trade may bring benefits by increasing scale economies, enhancing competition, transferring technology and increasing product diversity—all of which could *raise* wages of both high-school and college graduates. It also ignores the fact that poorer workers are more likely to consume the price-sensitive basic goods whose prices will fall as a result of trade. Moreover, once the economy eliminates domestic production of the basic industries in which the developing countries specialize, additional increases in world supplies of these products would *increase the real wages of all American workers* by providing them with cheaper imports.[20] Additional trade with developing countries would then not necessarily affect wage inequality in the United States (although given the relatively small overall shares of imported goods in consumption this effect should not be exaggerated). One implied message, therefore, is that while there may be some impact on inequality, in the long run, trade with developing countries should provide benefits to all who live in the OECD.

Finally, this simulation about the future also contains an implicit, but very important lesson about the past. If the impact of very large shifts in trade in the future is likely to be relatively small, it suggests that the much smaller growth in trade with developing countries over the past fifteen years is unlikely to have had the major impact on labor markets in the OECD countries which many claim it has.

F. CONCLUSIONS

In general the impact of globalization on the U.S. labor markets has been far less significant than many have argued. Trade played no role in the sluggish growth in average U.S. wages over the past two decades, a development which reflects the slowdown in U.S.

---

[20]If the developing countries shift into high-skill products, on the other hand, the U.S. terms of trade could decline.

productivity growth outside of manufacturing. Trade appears to have played some role, however, in employment shifts, particularly in the declining employment opportunities in labor-intensive sectors such as apparel. Nonetheless, as estimated by conventional net factor content methods, these effects remained too small to account for more than about ten to fifteen percent (i.e. 1.5 percentage points) of the differential that emerged between high-school and college workers in the United States. The minor role played by trade is also suggested by the behavior of the prices of traded goods in the 1980s. The negative relationship that might have been expected between import prices and the use of unskilled labor is not present in price data for the United States during the period in which the major increase in wage inequality was observed.

Nor is there evidence that trade operated on economy-wide relative wages by altering relative industry wage premiums on a large scale. In the United States specifically, workers with high-school degrees in high-rent industries (or union members) have experienced only minor declines in relative earnings. Nor has trade resulted in the erosion of sufficiently large numbers of high-rent jobs to have depressed the average (economy-wide) relative earnings of high-school graduates by reducing their employment in high-rent manufacturing sectors.

The evidence drawn from data on U.S. multinationals points to the dominant impact of a commonly shared technological change rather than the impact of trade and international outsourcing. Employment fell both in U.S. parents and in affiliates in developed countries and grew only modestly in developing countries. In foreign affiliates in both developed and developing countries, the relative compensation of non-production workers increased and the ratio of production to non-production workers fell—a result consistent with the argument of a pervasive shift in manufacturing production techniques which has increased the use and rewards of educated workers. While U.S. parent sourcing from overseas affiliates grew rapidly, the increase accounted for only a small share of total sales.

III. TRADE, EMPLOYMENT, AND WAGES: THE JAPANESE CASE

In many advanced countries globalization of markets has often been suspected as a cause of poor performance of labor markets, such as increased unemployment and/or wage inequality in recent years. This chapter will inquire whether and to what extent the issues raised are relevant in Japan, particularly focusing on their relationship to Japanese labor practices.

A. INTERNATIONALIZATION OF THE JAPANESE ECONOMY

Globalization

Much attention has already been paid by the Japanese public to the internationalization, or globalization, of the Japanese economy. However, Japan's reliance on foreign trade apparently is declining. The ratio of imports to GDP in nominal terms fell by half from 14.6 percent in 1980 to 7.2 percent in 1994, as shown in Table III-1. Notice that the ratio was low from the start in international comparison.[1] The ratio of exports to GDP also declined. Do these facts mean that Japan is exceptional in keeping its markets more closed than ever amidst the trend of overall globalization in the world? Not necessarily.

A different picture emerges when the figures are cited in real (instead of nominal) terms or the focus is on imports of manufactured goods. The ratio of imports to GDP in real terms rose from 8.3 percent in 1980 to 9.9 percent in 1994, in contrast to the fall in nominal terms. The ratio of imports of manufactured goods to domestic industrial output rose from 10.4 percent to 13.2 percent during the same period. The value of imports of manufactured goods increased from 32 billion dollars in 1980 to 152 billion dollars in 1994.

---

[1]Whether the low ratio of imports to GDP in Japan is due to the closedness of its markets has long been discussed. For a Japanese view, see Nakamura and Shibuya (1995).

TABLE III-1
Internationalization of the Japanese Economy

	1980	1985	1990	1994
Imports/GDP (nominal) (%)	14.6	11.1	10.0	7.2
Exports/GDP (nominal) (%)	13.7	14.5	10.7	9.3
Imports/GDP (real) (%)	8.3	7.3	10.0	9.9
Exports/GDP (real) (%)	9.5	11.6	10.7	11.9
Imports of manufactured goods (billion US$)	32	40	118	152
Imports of manufactured goods (as % of domestic industrial output)	10.4	10.2	14.1	13.2
Foreign direct investment (annual flow, million US$)	2,993	7,592	44,904	17,397
Offshore production (as % of domestic production)	2.3	3.0	6.4	7.4*
Current account/GDP (%)	-1.1	3.6	1.2	2.8

* 1993

The fall of the ratio of imports to GDP in nominal terms as well as its rise in real terms can partly be attributed to a sharp appreciation of the yen, which resulted partly from sustained surpluses in the current account of the Japanese balance of payments. The higher yen stimulated the penetration of foreign goods into the Japanese market in quantitative terms while reducing the value of imports measured in yen. Another factor that kept Japanese imports smaller was the stable prices of primary products during the 1980-94 period. Decreasing use of energy and natural resources as a reaction to the rise of their prices in the 1970s also contributed to some extent to the containment of imports.

With the appreciation of the yen, many Japanese firms shifted their production bases overseas and increased procurement from abroad. The annual flow of foreign direct investment overseas rose from 3 billion dollars in 1980 to 45 billion dollars in 1990, and recovered to a level of 17 billion dollars in 1994 after a sharp decline in the early 1990s. The ratio of offshore production of Japanese manufacturing industry increased from 2.3 percent in 1980 to 7.4 percent in 1993. Expanded foreign direct investment and a rise in offshore production provide a background for greater imports of consumer and intermediate goods into Japan.

Integration of global markets has brought about appreciation of the yen (which has decreased exports and increased imports in volume terms while decreasing the yen value of imports) and has encouraged Japanese firms to increase offshore production. In that sense, the Japanese economy is under the strong influence of globalization.

Looking at the details of import statistics (Tables III-2A, III-2B and III-2C), one finds that imports of manufactured goods in U.S. dollars from OECD countries increased by a factor of 3 from 1980 to 1993, while those from non-OECD countries increased by a factor of 5 during the same period. Among non-OECD countries, the dynamic Asian economies (DAEs) most conspicuously expanded their export of manufactured goods to Japan. Imports and import penetration ratios increased not only in light industries such as textiles, wooden products, and miscellaneous manufactured goods, but also in heavy or sophisticated intermediate and capital goods industries such as chemicals, iron and steel, and electronic machinery. Judging from the wide range of areas of origin and of commodities imported, the picture of imports solely of low-grade commodities from low-wage countries is too simplistic with respect to trade between Japan and Asia. The division of labor between Japan and Asia is developing not exclusively on an inter-industry basis but at least partially on an intra-industry level. The competition is taking place not only with low-wage countries but also with countries which are rapidly catching up technologically.

Public Concerns
There exists an apprehension that globalization of markets will give rise to a sea change in the economic conditions of Japan. Fear is widespread and often eloquently expressed that "hollowing out" of industries due to the expansion of offshore production might lead to massive unemployment. In wage negotiations, business firms insist that Japanese wages (measured in terms of dollars using the market

TABLE III-2A
Japanese Imports of Manufactured Goods

	1980	1985	1990	1993	'93/'80
	(billions of US$)				
From OECD Countries	19.34	23.86	70.48	66.39	3.43
From Non-OECD Countries	10.09	11.90	39.34	51.94	5.15

Source: OECD, *Foreign Trade by Commodities*

TABLE III-2B
Japan's Trade with DAEs and Big Three Combined
(billions of US$)

	1980	1985	1993
Total Manufactures			
exports	30.66	40.88	120.54
imports	5.33	8.06	43.41
exports minus imports	+25.33	+32.82	+77.12
Capital and Intermediate Goods			
exports	28.46	37.60	110.33
imports	3.31	5.01	24.67
exports minus imports	+25.15	+32.59	+85.66
Clothing			
exports	0.05	0.08	0.32
imports	1.07	1.64	9.89
exports minus imports	-1.02	-1.56	-9.57
Other Light Manufactures			
exports	2.15	3.20	9.89
imports	0.95	1.42	8.85
exports minus imports	+1.20	+1.79	+1.03

Source: OECD, *Foreign Trade by Commodities*
Notes: The dynamic Asian economies (DAEs) are South Korea, Taiwan, Hong Kong, Singapore, Malaysia and Thailand. The Big Three are China, India and Indonesia. "Capital and Intermediate Goods" are SITC 5, 6 and 7. "Clothing" is SITC 84. "Other Light Manufactures" are SITC 8. "Total Manufactures" are SITC 5, 6, 7 and 8.

TABLE III-2C
Japan's Manufactures Trade with Non-OECD Countries
(as percent of GDP)

	Exports	Imports	Surplus
1970	4.48	0.73	3.75
1975	6.31	0.68	5.63
1980	6.28	0.95	5.32
1985	5.23	0.89	4.34
1986	3.77	0.75	3.02
1987	3.46	0.94	2.51
1988	3.42	1.16	2.26
1989	3.58	1.36	2.22
1990	3.78	1.32	2.45
1991	3.89	1.31	2.58
1992	4.00	1.21	2.79
1993	3.89	1.21	2.68

Source: OECD, *Foreign Trade by Commodities*

exchange rate) are high compared to other industrial economies as well as to Japan's rapidly industrializing Asian neighbors. Labor unions argue that high wages in dollar terms at market exchange rates hide the still low living standard due to the high cost of living in Japan. Thus, however vaguely, their debate is centered upon the law of factor price equalization.

Some variation of emphasis from U.S. and EU concerns may be discerned in the Japanese way of thinking of the issues. The difference seems to be related to the particular economic conditions in Japan, where current surpluses remain huge and the exchange rate has appreciated. Apparently, the Japanese are more concerned about very low economic growth in recent years than about unemployment per se. The Japanese labor practice of life-time employment keeps unemployment under control for a while. But this might imply that adjustment is lagged, restructuring hampered, profits squeezed, and economic stagnation prolonged. It is feared that the life-time employment system may have to be broken some day if adjustment takes so much time.

The Japanese are more concerned with internal and international price differentials, i.e. the difference between the high value of the yen in exchange markets and its low purchasing power in domestic markets. The Purchasing Power Parity exchange rate in 1994 was 181 yen per dollar when the market exchange rate was 102 yen per dollar. This differential causes depressed living standards among the people as well as weakened competitiveness of industries, and drives firms to shift their production abroad.

The Japanese do not regard their new foreign competitors as unskilled and incompetent, relying only on their low wages. Rather, they regard them as rapidly improving their productivity, as was the case with the Japanese in the 1950s and 1960s. In other words, it is easier for the Japanese to imagine that international competition takes place not in low-tech areas, but rather in mid-tech sectors. The Japanese are concerned with technical change in connection with its impact on jobs and wages. At the same time, the effects of an aging population as well as of asset price deflation (which is still under way in Japan) cannot escape their attention.

B. LABOR MARKET PERFORMANCE

Employment

While Japan is becoming more or less globalized, its labor market performance gives a rather different impression from the United States or Europe. The current rate of unemployment is 3.4 percent in Japan, historically high according to Japanese standards, but definitely low compared to other countries. It is also amazing that Japan can keep its rate of unemployment so low after three years of virtually zero growth of the economy (1992-94). Surely there are several reasons why unemployment appears so low statistically in Japan:

(1) Many housewives and students in Japan report themselves not as unemployed but as outside the labor force, even when they are prepared to take part-time jobs if offered under favorable conditions. Although the boundary between those outside the labor force and those unemployed remains ambiguous everywhere, the rate of unemployment in Japan would increase to some extent—perhaps 2-3 percentage points—if all these "discouraged workers" counted outside the labor force were instead counted in the labor force as "unemployed."[2]

---

[2]The official figure for unemployment is based on the *Labor Force Survey* (monthly). More detailed questions about willingness to work are asked in the *Employment Status Survey* (every 5 years). Based on these two sources, although they are not exactly comparable, one can roughly estimate the size of such disguised unemployment. See Yashiro (1995a).

(2) The practice of so-called life-time employment, under which layoffs are rare, obliges business firms to retain excess labor within companies during recession. Another 2-3 percentage points would be added to the rate of unemployment if firms discharged these redundant workers from their shops and offices. For a detailed discussion of this phenomenon, see Yashiro (1995b).

(3) The supply of labor is increasing rather slowly. Hours worked are on a shrinking trend in Japan in contrast to the United States; immigration from abroad is severely restricted; and the population is aging far more rapidly in Japan than in other countries. The number of new college graduates reached a peak in March 1996. The absolute size of the working-age (15-64 years old) population will begin to decrease from 1996, but the labor force will still increase for a while thanks to higher participation of females. In addition, total population will begin to decline early in the twenty-first century. These current and expected demographic changes in Japan keep the unemployment rate relatively low.

The official figure of unemployment is far lower in Japan than in other advanced countries. If the disguised unemployment discussed in (1) and (2) above were to be added to the official estimate, however, it would reach 7–9 percent, a level which is not much different from those in the United States or in Europe. As long as families and firms retain the excess labor, families and firms bear the social cost of unemployment, and the unemployment problem is socially less serious. In that sense, Japan's labor market apparently performs rather well.

This, however, is not without its own problems. For example, under the life-time employment system firms refrain from firing older workers and restrain their hiring of new entrants; so difficulties are mounting for new college graduates to find appropriate jobs. More importantly, the hoarding of labor by Japanese firms has squeezed corporate profits, prolonged the recession, and delayed the industrial adjustment which is needed for globalization. There are apprehensions that unemployment will persist in the future, as restructuring of industries still has a long way to go. Thus, pressures for reforming Japanese labor practices to meet globalization are mounting in spite of their apparent success.

TABLE III-3
Average Monthly Wages and Wage Differentials in Japan

	Average Monthly Wages (1000 yen)			
	1980	1985	1990	1994
Manufacturing Industry				
male	193.3	238.4	278.1	317.0
female	102.7	125.8	149.9	175.5
45-49 years of age	189.6	243.6	294.2	333.7
20-24 years of age	113.0	135.8	159.4	182.6
college graduates	232.2	283.0	331.1	369.4
high school graduates	162.7	195.6	226.4	260.4
1000 employees of more	193.9	241.6	286.1	324.6
10-99 employees	146.4	178.4	209.7	241.1
non-production workers	202.2	247.8	289.0	328.1
production workers	146.0	178.6	207.7	238.5
Industries (overall average)	173.1	213.8	254.7	288.4
mining	181.2	222.2	261.4	293.6
manufacturing	166.1	204.0	240.1	276.7
construction	182.1	222.7	273.3	315.6
electricity and gas	220.9	276.4	332.8	376.1
transport	187.9	231.1	276.0	300.8
wholesale and retail trade	171.0	213.6	256.3	284.3
banking and insurance	198.1	258.0	308.4	334.7
real estate	193.9	236.6	276.7	314.6
services	168.0	205.4	244.2	280.7

Source: Ministry of Labor, *Census of Wages;* Management and Coordination Agency, *Annual Report on the Family Income and Expenditure Survey*

TABLE III-3 (continued)
Average Monthly Wages and Wage Differentials in Japan

	Wage Differentials			
	1980	1985	1990	1994
Manufacturing Industry				
male/ female	1.88	1.90	1.86	1.81
45-49 years of age/ 20-24 years of age	1.68	1.79	1.85	1.83
college graduates/ high school graduates	1.43	1.45	1.46	1.42
1000 employees of more/ 10-99 employees	1.32	1.35	1.36	1.35
non-production workers/ production workers	1.39	1.39	1.39	1.38
Industries (overall average)	1.000	1.000	1.000	1.000
mining	1.047	1.039	1.026	1.018
manufacturing	0.960	0.954	0.943	0.959
construction	1.052	1.042	1.073	1.094
electricity and gas	1.276	1.293	1.307	1.304
transport	1.085	1.081	1.084	1.043
wholesale and retail trade	0.988	0.999	1.006	0.986
banking and insurance	1.144	1.207	1.211	1.161
real estate	1.120	1.107	1.086	1.091
services	0.971	0.961	0.959	0.973
standard deviation	0.095	0.106	0.111	0.103
Wage dispersion among individuals*	1.00	1.08	1.12	1.10
Gini's coefficient				
all households	0.260	0.272	0.276	0.279
households of employees	0.219	0.227	0.227	0.224

* Wage dispersions are (90th percentile-10th percentile)/median of male workers in all industries.

Wages

In contrast with the U.S. experience, increasing wage inequality has not been so significant in Japan, particularly in the most recent years. Otake (1994) found that the income distribution inclusive of wages tended to become more unequal during the 1980s. However, in the years since 1990, while imports of manufactured goods increased in great strides and current account surpluses shrank significantly, the distribution of wage incomes became more equal again, judging by several indicators. According to the *Census of Wages*[3] by the Ministry of Labor (Table III-3), male-female wage differentials in manufacturing industries declined to 1.81 in 1994 from 1.90 in 1985, that of 45–49 year-olds to 20–24 year-olds to 1.83 in 1994 from 1.85 in 1990, that of college graduates to high school graduates to 1.42 in 1994 from 1.46 in 1990, that of large establishments (more than 1,000 persons employed) to smaller establishments (10–99 persons employed) to 1.35 in 1994 from 1.36 in 1990, and that of non-production workers to production workers to 1.38 in 1994 from 1.39 in 1985.[4] Wage dispersion among industries (measured in terms of standard deviation when the overall average is set equal to 1), after rising to 0.111 in 1990 from 0.095 in 1980, declined again to 0.103 in 1994.

These figures show smaller differentials of average wages between groups. They do not necessarily imply that wages are distributed more equally among individuals, as wage differentials within groups may expand over time. Turning to the numbers on wage dispersion among individuals, however, we find that the ratio of the difference of wages between the 90th percentile and the 10th percentile relative to the median of male workers in all industries remained almost unchanged in the past 10 years (1.08 in 1985, 1.12 in 1990 and 1.10 in 1994) according to the *Census of Wages*. According to the *Family Income and Expenditure Survey* by the Management and Coordination Agency of the Japanese Government, the Gini coefficient of income distribution among wage-earning families rose to 0.227 in 1985 and 1990 from 0.219 in 1980, but declined again to 0.224 in 1994.

---

[3]The *Census of Wages* (formally, the *Basic Survey on Wage Structure*) is an annual survey on wages of employees of private establishments based on a large sample (70 thousand establishments, 1.4 million employees). Notice, however, that it excludes (1) part-time workers and (2) enterprises with less than 9 employees, although data on enterprises with 5-9 employees are available with respect to some items. Wages in this chapter refer to "scheduled cash earnings" (Shoteinai kyuyo), unless otherwise specified.

[4]Wage differentials are mutually related so that a change in one differential affects another. However, wage differentials between college and high school graduates and between non-production and production workers would be smaller in 1994 than in 1985 even if age composition is fixed at 1985 levels. The former declined from 1.45 to 1.42, and the latter from 1.39 to 1.34.

Many indicators suggest a more unequal distribution of wages in 1990 than in 1980, but the movement towards inequality seems to have been halted or reversed in the 1990s. Some indicators suggest a more equal wage distribution in 1994 compared to 1990, to 1985, and a few even to 1980. One wonders how this tendency is related to pressure for reform of Japanese labor practices mentioned above.

C. TRADE, EMPLOYMENT, AND WAGES

In spite of the heightened public attention to the issue, only a few studies of the impact of globalization on the domestic labor market in Japan have appeared. In the following sections we examine in various ways the relationship between trade, employment, and wages in the Japanese case, following some of the preceding studies made in Japan as well as abroad.

Changes in Trade Structure Diminished Employment, Particularly of Less-Educated Workers

Tachibanaki et al (1995) studied the impact of external trade on employment using the employment multipliers of the aggregate demand components inclusive of exports and imports. The study is a simplified version of the inter-industry analysis made by Sachs and Shatz (1994). In what follows we construct a counterfactual scenario similar to that of Sachs and Shatz, from Japanese data, relying on the input-output tables of 32 industries compiled by the Nikkei Databank.[5]

The following steps are taken: (1) We define the sectoral export and import coefficients as the ratio of sectoral exports and imports to domestic final demand in that sector.[6] (2) We construct counterfactual exports and imports in 1994 by multiplying the export and import coefficients of 1980 by domestic final demand in 1994. (3) Actual domestic final demand is added to the counterfactual net exports thus obtained to calculate counterfactual final demand for 1994. (4) Counterfactual intermediate demand and total output in 1994 are calculated by using counterfactual final demand and the inverse

---

[5]The Japanese government (Management and Coordination Agency) publishes detailed input-output tables every five years. The latest version is for 1990. The annual input-output table in concise form is prepared by the Ministry of International Trade and Industry as well as by Nikkei Databank. The Nikkei Databank table is used here as its edition for 1994 was available when we were preparing this chapter.

[6]Sachs and Shatz (1994) define the coefficients as the ratios to final demand. We adopted domestic final demand instead of final demand in order to avoid some anomalies.

matrix of input coefficients of the respective years. (5) Multiplying the respective sectoral employment coefficients by the respective industries' gross output, we obtain counterfactual employment in 1994—i.e., employment if export and import coefficients had remained the same in 1994 as they were in 1980. (6) Employment in each sector of industry is classified according to school years of employees, relying on the *Census of Wages* by the Ministry of Labor. (7) Actual employment in 1994 is compared to counterfactual employment for the same year.

Table III-4 shows that the employment in 1994 would have been 3.0 percent greater than it actually was in 1994 if export and import coefficients had remained unchanged from 1980. In other words, changes in trade structure diminished employment to that extent. The loss of employment due to imports (again, measured in terms of the difference between counterfactual and actual employment) was 3.9 percent. However, the changes in the propensities to export caused a 0.9 percent gain of employment.

TABLE III-4
Employment Effects of Changes in Trade Structure, 1980-94

	All Workers	HS	COL
All Industries			
Net Effect	+3.0	+3.6	+1.9
Exports	-0.9	-0.7	-1.2
Imports	+3.9	+4.3	+3.1
Manufacturing			
Net Effect	+10.9	+11.4	+9.1
Exports	+0.1	+0.3	-0.7
Imports	+10.8	+11.1	+9.8

Note: Counterfactual employment in 1994 has been constructed using the 1980 trade structure. Actual employment in 1994 has then been subtracted from counterfactual employment, and the difference taken as a percentage of actual employment in 1994. Thus a positive number in this table indicates that actual employment in 1994 is less than it would have been with the 1980 trade structure, while a negative number indicates that actual employment is higher. HS = workers with high school education or less. COL = workers with at least some college education.

TABLE III-5
**Distribution of Employment Losses
and Gains Among Sectors**

	Net Effect	Exports	Imports
Employment Change	1,550,000	-440,000	1,980,000
Distribution Among Sectors (%)			
Agriculture	1.9	0.3	1.4
Mining	1.9	0.2	1.5
Food	8.4	-0.2	6.6
Textiles & Apparel	31.8	28.3	18.6
Paper & Furniture	6.1	-1.7	5.2
Chemicals	1.3	-9.1	3.0
Petroleum & Coal	0.1	-0.2	0.1
Stone & Ceramics	2.4	4.8	0.8
Steel	2.1	1.8	1.3
Nonferrous Metals	5.1	8.2	2.2
Metal Products	7.7	17.0	2.3
General Machinery	-4.3	-26.5	2.5
Electric Machinery	-20.2	-104.9	7.3
Transportation Machinery	-1.7	-17.8	2.6
Precision Machinery	34.5	111.4	2.5
Miscellaneous Manufactures	9.1	-8.1	8.9
Construction	0.8	-0.8	0.8
Electricity & Gas	0.5	-0.4	0.5
Water & Waste Disposal	0.4	-0.4	0.4
Wholesale & Retail Trade	-3.1	-41.3	6.7
Banking & Insurance	3.0	-2.1	2.8
Real Estate	0.1	-0.3	0.2
Transportation	1.4	-7.7	2.8
Communication	0.6	-1.5	0.8
Public	0.4	0.2	0.3
Education & Research	-0.3	-20.5	4.3
Medical & Other Public Services	0.1	-1.1	0.3
Business Services	9.8	-27.5	13.7
Business Services	6.6	-20.6	9.7
Personal Services	3.2	-6.9	4.0
Total	100.0%	100.0%	100.0%

Note: This table is an elaboration of the exercise summarized in Table III-4. Actual employment in 1994 has been subtracted from counterfactual employment. The overall loss (+) of employment due to imports is 1,980,000 according to this calculation. The overall gain (-) due to changes in propensities to export is 440,000 according to this calculation. The net effect, therefore, is that counterfactual employment is 1,550,000 higher than actual employment. The balance of this table distributes these employment losses and gains by sector. A positive number indicates an employment loss; a negative number an employment gain.

The distribution of employment losses among sectors is shown in Table III-5. The loss due to imports was large in textiles and apparel, miscellaneous manufacturing, and electrical machinery. The loss in business services should not be overlooked. The gain due to exports was large in electric machinery, general machinery, transportation machinery, wholesale and retail trade, business services, and research and education, while exports caused the large loss of employment in precision machinery, textiles and apparel, and metal products. As a result of the total effect of net exports, precision machinery showed a large loss. On the other hand, electrical machinery gained substantially from net exports.

By allocating the losses and gains in employment due to imports and exports into categories of employment, the differentiated effects of external trade on employment become apparent. Table III-4 suggests that the change of trade structure in 1980-94 has affected more adversely the employment of high school graduates rather than that of college graduates, although employment of both high school graduates and college graduates was diminished due to the changes in foreign trade structure during the above-mentioned period. This seems justifiable from the viewpoint of traditional trade theory which regards educated labor as a relatively abundant factor of production in advanced nations including Japan.

Relative Wages of College-Educated Workers Generally Declined (while Employment Ratio Generally Increased)

Such differentiated effects of trade on employment are sometimes cited and discussed as a plausible explanation for the widening wage disparity between educated and less-educated labor in the United States and in the European Union. To what extent the explanation applies must be further examined by looking into wage developments in Japan.

Much attention has been paid to the widening wage differentials between skilled and unskilled labor in the United States. As was discussed by Lawrence and Slaughter (1993), if this increased wage inequality is due to the working of the theorem of factor price equalization, the ratio of skilled/unskilled (educated/less educated or non-production/production) labor in every branch of industry (that is, in skilled-labor-intensive as well as unskilled-labor-intensive sectors) should be lower after market opening. In other words, changes in relative wages and in the composition of the labor force should be negatively related. But Lawrence and Slaughter found the opposite.

The Economic Planning Agency of the Japanese Government in its annual economic survey (EPA 1995) put the Japanese data to the same kind of test. This survey also found that wages of non-production (supervisory, technical, and clerical, as a proxy of skilled) workers rose relative to those of production workers from 1985 to 1993 across many branches of manufacturing industry (although marginally) and that the ratios of non-production to production workers also rose in a majority of branches, thus agreeing with Lawrence and Slaughter and denying the working of factor price equalization.

We have repeated the test by (1) changing the end year of observation from 1993 to 1994, and (2) adding the classification of educated (college graduates)/less-educated (high school graduates) workers to that of non-production/production workers.

Before discussing the test, however, it must be noted that we are faced with a puzzle. In previous studies of the United States, widening wage inequality has been at the heart of the issue. But as was shown in Table III-3, wage differentials have not been enlarged but narrowed in Japan. We will return to this point after looking through the results of the test.

In almost every branch of manufacturing industries under our observation, the ratio of educated to less-educated workers rose, while the relative wages of the former declined (although marginally) in 1994 compared to 1985 (Figure III-1). When the employment ratio is taken along the X-axis and the relative wages along the Y-axis, every point is located in the lower-right quadrant, instead of in the upper-right quadrant as was the case with Lawrence and Slaughter and the EPA. This appears to contradict not only the usual assumption of factor price equalization (in which points should be located in the upper-left quadrant) but also the counter-claim of skilled-labor-biased technical progress (which is consistent with points located in the upper-right quadrant). With factor price equalization, the ratio of skilled to unskilled labor should decrease while the relative wages of skilled labor rise. With skilled-labor-biased technical progress, skilled labor should be both more extensively used and better paid.

In Japan, wages of non-production workers relative to production workers in manufacturing industries declined in 1994 compared to 1985, as Table III-3 above showed. In many branches relative wages of non-production workers declined while their share among employees increased. Many points in Figure III-2 fall in the lower-right quadrant, as was the case with all points in Figure III-1. The results are not in

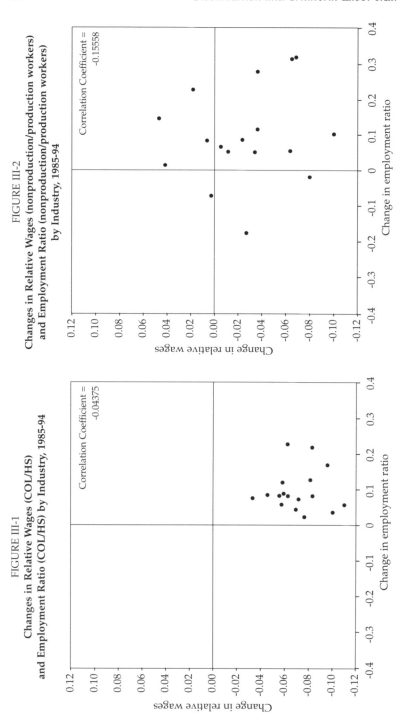

FIGURE III-2

Changes in Relative Wages (nonproduction/production workers) and Employment Ratio (nonproduction/production workers) by Industry, 1985-94

Correlation Coefficient = -0.15558

Source: Ministry of Labor, *Census of Wages*

Note: Nonproduction workers include supervisory, clerical and technical workers. The points in this figure are more scattered than in Figure III-1, but for 10 of the 17 industries covered by the data, the ratio of nonproduction workers to production workers increased between 1985 and 1994, while the wages of nonpro-

FIGURE III-1

Changes in Relative Wages (COL/HS) and Employment Ratio (COL/HS) by Industry, 1985-94

Correlation Coefficient = -0.04375

Source: Ministry of Labor, *Census of Wages*

Note: COL = college graduates; HS = high school graduates. All points are in the lower-right quadrant in this figure, indicating that, for each of the 17 industries covered by the data, the ratio of college workers to high school workers increased between 1985 and 1994, while the wages of college workers relative to the wages

accordance with the usual expectation of factor price equalization, nor with the preceding studies.

Minford et al (1995) emphasize the importance of using a detailed industrial classification in discussing the effects of trade on employment. They found that a negative relationship between changes in relative wages and labor composition emerges if one uses three-digit instead of two-digit industrial classifications. Although there is no figure reported on the basis of three-digit classifications in the *Census of Wages*, classification of two-digit industries into three classes by the size of enterprises (more than 1,000, 100-999, and 10-99 employees respectively) is available. Exercises based on the latter type of data show increased negative correlation between changes in relative wages and in labor composition when college and high-school graduates are compared, but the sign is reversed with respect to non-production/production workers. The values of correlation coefficients remain low in any case (Figures III-3 and III-4).[7]

One should not draw any hasty conclusions when relative wages change direction when one adds data for one year or changes the proxy for skilled labor slightly. However, the decline (however marginal) of relative wages of college graduates from 1985 to 1994 is apparently inconsistent with our former estimation that the employment of college graduates was less adversely affected by foreign trade. It also casts a doubt on the supposition that factor price equalization is working dominantly in Japan during the observed period. On the other hand, the counterclaim that technological progress is biased toward more intensive use of skilled labor is not fully affirmed either.

Why Has Wage Dispersion Narrowed Amidst Globalization?
Some conjectures why wage dispersion has been narrowed amidst globalization in Japan are as follows:

Supply Shift. Suppose that demand shifts toward use of skilled labor (reflecting biased technical progress, for example). It seems natural to expect that their relative wages will increase together with their employment. When relative wages decline while use increases, as in Figures III-1 and III-2, it is natural to expect that a supply shift toward skilled labor is more important than the demand shift.

---

[7]Another way to test whether factor price equalization holds is to regress skill intensity on price changes (Sachs and Shatz 1994, EPA 1995, and Lawrence 1996a). We regressed skill intensity of manufacturing industries in 1985 on changes in GDP deflators by industry between 1985 and 1994. The result was very poor (the coefficient is negative but not significant, and R2=0.015).

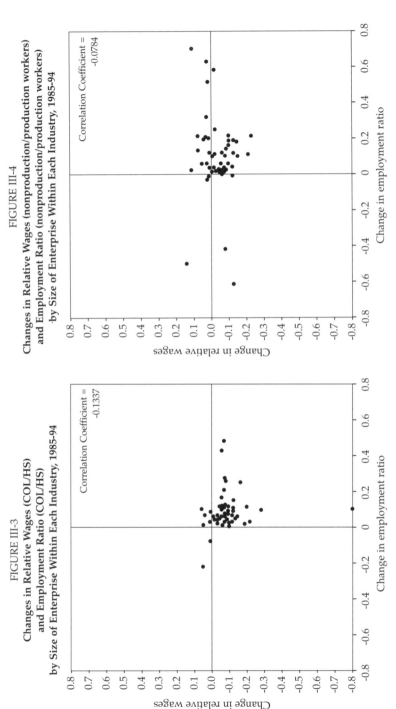

FIGURE III-4

Changes in Relative Wages (nonproduction/production workers) and Employment Ratio (nonproduction/production workers) by Size of Enterprise Within Each Industry, 1985-94

Correlation Coefficient = -0.0784

Change in relative wages

Change in employment ratio

Source: Ministry of Labor, *Census of Wages*

Note: Nonproduction workers include supervisory, clerical and technical workers. Enterprises have been broken down into three size categories (more than 1000 employees, 100-999 employees, 10-99 employees) within each industry. The points in this figure are more scattered than in Figure III-2 with-

FIGURE III-3

Changes in Relative Wages (COL/HS) and Employment Ratio (COL/HS) by Size of Enterprise Within Each Industry, 1985-94

Correlation Coefficient = -0.1337

Change in relative wages

Change in employment ratio

Source: Ministry of Labor, *Census of Wages*

Note: COL = college graduates; HS = high school graduates. Enterprises have been broken down into three size categories (more than 1000 employees, 100-999 employees, 10-99 employees) within each industry. Not all points (as in Figure III-1 without the size breakdown) are in the lower-right quadrant in

As far as education is concerned, supply is definitely shifting over time. The percentage of college graduates among people 60-64 years old in 1990 was 10.4 percent, while that among 20–24 years old (including those attending college) was 47.1 percent, according to the *Census of Population*. As the years proceed and worker replacement continues, the ratio of college graduates to high school graduates increases. The absolute number of high school graduates in all industries and in manufacturing industries fell from 16,469 (thousand persons) and 7,050 in 1980 to 15,651 and 6,137 in 1994, while that of college graduates rose from 3,836 and 1,064 to 7,497 and 1,856 during the same period, according to the *Census of Wages*. Changes in supply of college and high school graduates may have outpaced the changes in demand for them induced by trade or by technology. There seems to be some possibility that the ratio of non-production and production workers may be influenced by the changing share of college graduates among workers. The absolute number of production workers in manufacturing decreased from 5,279 (thousand persons) in 1980 to 4,582 in 1994.

Effects of Recession in Finance and Real Estate. The recent decline in relative wages of educated labor may well be explained by the current recession in finance and real estate, which used to be educated-labor-intensive sectors. After the burst of the economic bubble in the early 1990s, these sectors have been suffering severely from bad loans and a sluggish market. Relative wages in these industrial sectors were depressed, as shown in Table III-3. This sectoral distress might affect wages of college graduates adversely across all sectors. As long as the slumps in these sectors are of a cyclical nature, the current change in relative wages may be temporary.

One may, however, venture to speculate that the recession in finance and real estate is not unrelated to the working of factor price equalization. The recession was caused by the crash in land prices. The price of land fell because the expectations that Tokyo would become a global financial center and that office buildings in Tokyo would be in excess demand as foreign and domestic finance companies came and settled in Tokyo were betrayed, partly because land prices in Tokyo were already too high. In an era of high capital mobility, factor price equalization occurs not only through trade but also through the location of offices. Locational competition thus directly affects the price of land. Since college graduates are complementary inputs to land (or more accurately to office space), the fall of land prices as a result of factor price equalization brings about the fall of relative wages of college graduates.

Deregulation. Some regulated industries such as finance, telecommunications, and electricity also use educated labor intensively. They enjoy a monopoly and protection and are willing to pay high wages to their employees, who consist mostly of college graduates. High wages for college graduates in protected non-manufacturing domestic industries affect those of tradable manufacturing industries so as to keep college graduates' relative wages higher than otherwise. Deregulation destroys the market power of formerly regulated industries. The workers in these sectors are deprived of their share of monopoly premiums. The loss also affects wages in other sectors, and the effects will be stronger for educated labor than for less-educated labor as these sectors use educated labor intensively. Deregulation of finance, telecommunications, and electricity is among the hot issues in Japan today.

Deregulation of domestic industries is not totally unrelated to the globalization of markets. Deregulation is requested by other countries in order to open markets and level the playing field. Finance and information industries compete fiercely across borders nowadays. Regulation of domestic industries apparently contributes to inefficiency and high costs, which are in turn conducive to wide discrepancies between domestic and international prices for Japanese, as mentioned above. The internal and external price differentials are not only resented by Japanese consumers, but also make it difficult for Japanese and foreign firms to invest in Japan. In that sense deregulation is a way to bring about factor price equalization broadly interpreted.

Reforms in Seniority Wages. Japanese firms have to retain excess labor during a recession under life-time employment practices. This squeezes their profits, and makes their industrial adjustment more difficult. Transformation of Japanese labor practices so as to constrain wage-bills and to heighten labor mobility is earnestly called for. The need to restrain the salaries of middle-aged white-collar workers has so far been particularly emphasized. Introduction of an annual salary system as well as of pay based on competence rather than seniority has been proposed and experimented with for middle-management white-collar employees. The move, which sometimes takes the form of "white-collar bashing," appears to have contributed to a narrowing of wage inequality so far.

There seem to be several reasons why the reform is targeted toward wages of white-collar employees in Japan. Perhaps they are chosen as a target because they are not members of trade unions. During the bubble years of the late 1980s the share of non-production workers among total employees in manufacturing industries increased remarkably, based on the expectation that they would be in greater demand in the information age. Perhaps, they are now thought to be redundant as innovations in information technology will replace them.[8]

The decline in the expected rate of growth combined with the aging of the workforce appear important among other factors as an impetus for reforming seniority wages. Firms are now faced with an increase of wage bills amidst slower growth, due to the rapid aging of the workforce under the life-time employment and seniority wage systems. The age-wage profile must be amended as long as life-time employment is maintained. Seniority wages are more conspicuous among college graduates, or among white-collar employees in the middle-management stratum, than among high school graduates, or among production workers. It is natural that the reform of seniority wages is targeted at the former class of employees. Rather ironically, a side effect is narrower wage inequality.

According to a recent survey (Nikkeiren 1994), Japanese firms have different views as to the elements of Japanese labor practices. Eighty-one percent of Japanese firms prefer to retain enterprise-based trade unions, and 38 percent of them prefer to maintain long-term employment practices, while 97 percent of them expect changes in seniority wages. The three pillars of Japanese labor practices—that is, enterprise-based unions, long-term employment, and seniority wages—have so far been regarded as intertwined, inseparable, or institutionally complementary. However, they are now to be treated more or less separately.

How far the reform could go still remains to be seen, however. Under the seniority wage system, it is generally supposed that younger employees receive less than they contribute after the initial training period in the expectation that later they will receive more than they contribute, as their elders currently receive more than they contribute. If so, firms will benefit by cutting the wages of aged workers without damaging productivity at least in the short run. However, changes in age-wage profiles may well destroy this expectation and be resented by employees as a betrayal of implicit

---

[8]On the contrary, Krueger (1993) asserts that the use of computers raised relative wages of college graduates considerably. To my knowledge, there is no counterpart study on this issue based on Japanese data.

contracts. On the other hand, employees may accept lower-than-expected wages as a cost of maintaining life-time employment under changed economic and demographic conditions. It will take time for any adjustments in long-term employment practices and appropriate age-wage profiles to be agreed upon between labor and management. The reforms in Japanese labor practices are still in the beginning stage, and their effects on social peace, stability, long-run incentives for productivity improvements, and flexibility to adjustment must be carefully watched, analyzed, and taken into consideration in the future course of reform.

Productivity of White-Collar Employees. The aging population is not the sole reason for reforming labor practices in Japan. Productivity also matters. According to the survey made by Shakai Keizai Seisansei Honbu (1994), 50 percent of Japanese firms regard the productivity of Japanese white-collar employees as inferior to that of white-collar workers in other advanced nations, while 70 percent of Japanese firms regard it as lower than that of Japanese blue-collar workers. Japanese industries have tried and succeeded in improving productivity on the shop-floor. All of the techniques to promote efficiency developed in Japan, inclusive of lean production, just-in-time inventory management, small group activities, and employees' proposals, are concerned with manufacturing processes in the narrow sense. On the contrary, decision-making in Japanese management based on consensus formation from below (in which white-collar employees are mainly engaged) is regarded as inefficient, slow, and time-consuming, since complicated processes of organization coordination (*nemawasi*) are necessary. Productivity improvements in office operations have been left aside.[9] With such a perception,[10] although not well-analyzed statistically so far (see Yamagami [1993 and 1994] for critical comments on conventional views), the downward pressures on wages of white-collar workers developed.

The productivity issue leads us to more speculation that might reconcile the observed movement in relative wages with factor price

---

[9]As circumstantial evidence for low productivity of managerial workers in Japan, the low utilization of personal computers, small numbers of personal computers connected with LAN, and small size of the market for databases are sometimes quoted.

[10]The perception that productivity is high in branches directly related to production activities while low in managerial or indirect branches in the Japanese firms roughly corresponds to the view that productivity is high in manufacturing industries and low in service and distribution industries in the Japanese economy. The latter view is often cited as a cause of wide discrepancies in external and internal prices for Japanese.

equalization. It may well be that high school graduates or production workers are more efficient resources in Japan than college graduates and non-production workers. Japan's comparative advantage then lies on the shop-floor of manufacturing industries, not in laboratories or offices. If this interpretation is right, the changes in relative wages in Japan are not surprising at all. If so, however, it is implicitly assumed that Japan lags behind other advanced countries in symbol analysis in particular or in knowledge-intensive information technology in general. Whether this hypothesis is supported by facts or not is to be further explored.

If the relative wages of college graduates had been extremely high in Japan from the start, as Japan is in comparative perspective a newly industrialized country, their decline is natural also as a result of factor price equalization. However, this assumption does not hold. According to the OECD (1994, Table 7.1), wage differentials among workers with different educational attainments were smaller in Japan than other OECD countries in the early 1970s, and were even smaller in the early 1990s.

Again, if the share of white-collar workers among employees was high in Japan compared to other countries from the start, it is easier to understand the decline of their relative wages. This is not the case, however. In 1990, the share of high school graduates among total employees in manufacturing industries was 83 percent in Japan (see Table III-10), much higher than in the United States (see Table II-4).

Wage Premiums

Borjas and Ramey (1993) presented another explanation for wider wage inequality in the United States. The title of their paper—"Foreign Competition, Market Power, and Wage Inequality"—succinctly summarizes their story. That is, foreign competition brought about wage inequality by destroying market power and diminishing industrial rents. One may wonder why a good thing (competition, destruction of market power) brings a bad thing (wage inequality), or whether it is worthwhile to protect the industrial rents shared by a privileged class of workers. Without attempting such a welfare judgment, we will examine the changes in industrial rents contained in wages in respective industries in Japan in connection with trends in foreign trade.

Tachibanaki (1992) estimated the rent components (or industry premium) of wages of respective branches of the Japanese

TABLE III-6
**Estimated Natural Log Wage Differentials between Workers
in Japanese Industries**

		Total Workers		
		1979	1990	1994
1.	Mining	-0.018	-0.036	-0.017
2.	Food	-0.114	-0.148	-0.135
3.	Textiles & Apparel	-0.180	-0.225	-0.246
4.	Paper & Furniture	-0.120	-0.130	-0.125
5.	Chemicals	0.049	0.067	0.037
6.	Petroleum & Coal	0.078		
7.	Stone & Ceramics	-0.056	-0.078	-0.069
8.	Steel	0.060	0.014	-0.003
9.	Nonferrous Metals	-0.023	-0.045	-0.061
10.	Metal Products	-0.035	-0.051	-0.040
11.	General Machinery	-0.024	-0.026	-0.032
12.	Electric Machinery	-0.086	-0.096	-0.078
13.	Transportation Machinery	0.097	-0.017	-0.018
14.	Precision Machinery	-0.038	-0.057	-0.072
15.	Miscellaneous Manufacturing	-0.015	-0.002	-0.008
16.	Construction	0.009	0.019	0.056
17.	Public Utilities	0.081	0.148	0.140
18.	Waste Disposal		0.089	0.124
19.	Wholesale & Retail Trade	-0.046	-0.065	-0.078
20.	Banking & Insurance	0.194	0.278	0.183
21.	Real Estate	0.153	0.151	0.120
22.	Transportation	-0.016	-0.037	-0.057
23.	Communication			0.104
24.	Services	0.050		
24a.	Education & Research		0.144	0.131
24b.	Medical Services		0.156	0.168
24c.	Business Services		0.005	0.014
24d.	Personal Services		-0.058	-0.040
	Sample Size	748	1273	1274
	Weighted adjusted standard deviation of differentials (weighted by employment shares)	0.088	0.115	0.101

Source: Ministry of Labor, *Census of Wages*

TABLE III-6 (continued)
**Estimated Natural Log Wage Differentials between Workers
in Japanese Industries**

	HS (workers with high school education or less)			COL (workers with some college education)		
	1979	1990	1994	1979	1990	1994
1.	-0.023	-0.054	-0.037	0.060	0.085	0.088
2.	-0.119	-0.153	-0.142	-0.076	-0.100	-0.086
3.	-0.186	-0.231	-0.253	-0.089	-0.110	-0.106
4.	-0.122	-0.136	-0.132	-0.095	-0.091	-0.086
5.	0.050	0.055	0.028	0.053	0.099	0.045
6.	0.073			0.095		
7.	-0.058	-0.084	-0.072	-0.047	-0.042	-0.065
8.	0.061	-0.003	-0.022	0.075	0.085	0.048
9.	-0.025	-0.055	-0.075	-0.009	-0.011	-0.022
10.	-0.034	-0.049	-0.035	-0.067	-0.078	-0.063
11.	-0.019	-0.025	-0.026	-0.047	-0.041	-0.051
12.	-0.094	-0.105	-0.086	-0.062	-0.059	-0.047
13.	0.106	-0.011	-0.009	0.043	-0.037	-0.043
14.	-0.034	-0.052	-0.071	-0.070	-0.078	-0.066
15.	-0.021	-0.010	-0.023	0.021	0.023	0.029
16.	0.018	0.030	0.066	-0.071	-0.017	0.022
17.	0.099	0.149	0.148	0.026	0.112	0.074
18.		0.121	0.150		-0.025	0.088
19.	-0.038	-0.039	-0.047	-0.114	-0.138	-0.131
20.	0.232	0.372	0.272	0.089	0.149	0.102
21.	0.150	0.173	0.139	0.151	0.085	0.083
22.	-0.012	-0.035	-0.055	-0.047	-0.068	-0.086
23.			0.108			0.068
24.	0.004			0.181		
24a.		0.094	0.073		0.163	0.135
24b.		0.107	0.129		0.206	0.194
24c.		-0.019	-0.009		0.019	0.036
24d.		-0.039	-0.020		-0.129	-0.080
	464	705	684	284	568	590
	0.100	0.103	0.072	0.103	0.111	0.097

Notes: This table uses basic monthly wages without any additional allowances. Controls include log of years of service, a female dummy, three firm-size dummies and four education dummies.

manufacturing industry, utilizing 34,000 samples from the _Census of Wages_ in 1978 and 1988, following the estimation for American industries by Katz and Summers (1989). We estimated, basically in the same way, wage premiums of Japanese industries in 1979, 1990, and 1994 (Table III-6). We used (instead of a large micro data set) aggregate figures from the published tables in the _Census of Wages_, and controlled such characteristics as sex, level of education, working years, and size of establishments.

Table III-7 shows that the values of the coefficients of most controlling variables diminished between 1979 and 1994. This may be more direct evidence of narrowing wage inequality than the difference in average wages of the respective categories of workers. (The exception is "4 years or more" of college, which also tips upward "some college education" between 1990 and 1994.) Changes in coefficients show changes in "pure" differences in wages originating respectively from sex, age, school years, occupation, and size of enterprises. The results here confirm that wage differences have generally been shrinking in recent years.

Industrial premiums in 1990 are compared to unionization ratios and regulation ratios in Tables III-8A and III-8B and Figures III-5A

TABLE III-7
Estimated Natural Log Wage Differentials among Types of Workers

	1979	1990	1994
Male	0.342	0.375	0.327
Some College Education	0.208	0.172	0.177
2 years	0.169	0.075	0.071
4 years or more	0.220	0.226	0.238
Size of Enterprise			
100-999 employees	0.054	0.064	0.048
1000 or more employees	0.181	0.214	0.150

Note: Above figures are estimated parameters to the dummy variables of the same equations as in Table III-6. Null of male dummy is female, null of college education is high school, and null of enterprise sizes is 99 employees or less.

TABLE III-8A
Labor Union Participation Rate by Industry, 1990

	Union Members	Total Employees	Participation Rate (%)
Agriculture	54,743	465,014	11.8
Mining	17,686	85,795	20.6
Food	250,995	1,491,730	16.8
Textiles & Apparel	213,992	1,104,074	19.4
Paper & Furniture	139,442	826,245	16.9
Chemicals	340,957	490,616	69.5
Petroleum & Coal	24,937	46,388	53.8
Stone & Ceramics	131,272	256,431	51.2
Steel	219,270	374,334	58.6
Nonferrous Metals	109,426	163,807	66.8
Metal Products	155,768	1,012,400	15.4
General Machinery	342,691	1,159,922	29.5
Electric Machinery	862,026	1,873,998	46.0
Transportation Machinery	698,518	1,033,036	67.6
Precision Machinery	138,242	250,541	55.2
Miscellaneous Manufactures	312,075	1,512,220	20.6
Construction	841,042	4,537,884	18.5
Public Utilities	170,039	206,677	82.3
Waste Disposal	103,294	336,847	30.7
Wholesale & Retail Trade	1,057,369	9,696,307	10.9
Banking & Insurance	1,126,552	2,069,851	54.4
Real Estate	17,430	404,114	4.3
Transportation	1,208,421	2,644,581	45.7
Communication	479,877	606,773	79.1
Services	1,819,855	13,141,796	13.8
Public Services	1,321,636	1,920,089	68.8
Firm Size (private firms)			
1000 persons and over	4,150,288	9,070,000	45.8
500-999 persons	2,100,618	2,420,000	86.8
100-499 persons	4,228,895	7,760,000	54.5
30-99 persons	1,386,626	7,710,000	18.0
1-29 persons	326,969	15,890,000	2.1

Source: Ministry of Labor, *Labor Union Survey*; Statistics Bureau, Management and Coordination Agency, *Labor Force Survey* and *Input-Output Tables*

TABLE III-8B
Regulation Ratio by Industry, 1989

	Regulation Ratio A	Regulation Ratio B
Mining	1	0.718
Food	0.33	0.192
Textiles & Apparel	0.556	0.33
Chemicals	0.253	0.147
Steel	0	0
Nonferrous Metals	0	0
Metal Products	0	0
Machinery	0.052	0.03
Construction	1	0
Public Utilities	1	1
Banking & Insurance	1	1
Real Estate	0.036	0.036
Transportation	0.953	0.909
Services	0.545	0.241

Source: Planning Bureau, Economic Planning Agency, *Gendai no Rakuichi Rakuza—Kisei Kanwa to Keizai Kasseika* (Contemporary Free Markets—Deregulation and Revitalization of the Economy), 1995, p. 79, Table 3-6.

Notes: Regulation Ratio A refers to the share of branches of the respective sector which are under at least one of the following forms of regulation: entry control, volume control (inclusive of control on equipment size), or price control. Regulation Ratio B refers to the share of branches of the respective sector which, in addition to entry control, are under volume and/or price control. Regulation Ratio B is used in the text of this chapter and in plotting Figure III-5B.

and III-5B. It appears that highly organized sectors tend to enjoy higher premiums. The coefficient of correlation between the two is 0.274. The regulation ratios used here are a far-from-exact index (for the definition, see the notes to Table III-8B and Figure III-5B), as regulation is multidimensional and not easy to measure in scope and intensity. Still, the statement with regard to unionization apparently holds for regulation as well. The coefficient of correlation between industrial premiums and regulation ratios is 0.372, suggesting that industrial premiums tend to be higher in strictly regulated sectors.

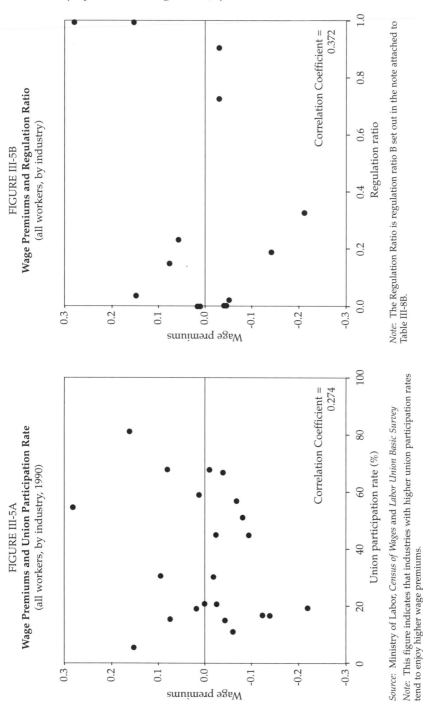

FIGURE III-5A
Wage Premiums and Union Participation Rate
(all workers, by industry, 1990)

FIGURE III-5B
Wage Premiums and Regulation Ratio
(all workers, by industry)

Correlation Coefficient = 0.274

Correlation Coefficient = 0.372

Union participation rate (%)

Regulation ratio

Source: Ministry of Labor, *Census of Wages and Labor Union Basic Survey*
Note: This figure indicates that industries with higher union participation rates tend to enjoy higher wage premiums.

Note: The Regulation Ratio is regulation ratio B set out in the note attached to Table III-8B.

TABLE III-9
**Foreign Trade Ratio to Final Demand
and Wage Premiums**

		exports/ final demand		imports/ final demand		change in trade ratio (exp)	(imp)
		1980	1994	1980	1994	94/80	94/80
1.	Mining	0.00	0.00	-1.01	-1.00	0.24	-0.01
2.	Food	0.02	0.01	0.11	0.22	-0.54	1.03
3.	Textiles & Apparel	0.18	0.13	0.12	0.69	-0.28	4.72
4.	Paper & Furniture	0.22	0.25	0.82	1.58	0.11	0.93
5.	Chemicals	0.69	0.85	0.45	0.72	0.24	0.60
6.	Stone & Ceramics	0.75	1.06	0.22	0.94	0.41	3.20
7.	Steel	1.28	1.58	0.13	0.48	0.23	2.66
8.	Nonferrous Metals	-8.78	-0.46	-11.90	-1.63	-0.95	-0.86
9.	Metal Products	0.48	0.37	0.05	0.29	-0.23	4.83
10.	General Machinery	0.33	0.38	0.06	0.10	0.17	0.57
11.	Electric Machinery	0.37	0.50	0.06	0.15	0.35	1.36
12.	Transportation Machinery	0.53	0.49	0.04	0.11	-0.07	1.43
13.	Precision Machinery	0.47	0.59	0.16	0.45	0.25	1.89
14.	Miscellaneous Manufact'g	0.18	0.23	0.16	0.57	0.25	2.58
15.	Construction	0.00	0.00	0.00	0.00	0.00	0.00
16.	Public Utilities	0.00	0.00	0.00	0.00	1.06	-0.34
17.	Waste Disposal	0.00	0.00	0.00	0.00		
18.	Wholesale & Retail Trade	0.07	0.04	0.02	0.01	-0.50	-0.75
19.	Banking & Insurance	0.08	0.04	0.09	0.06	-0.52	-0.32
20.	Real Estate	0.00	0.00	0.00	0.00	-0.57	0.59
21.	Transportation	0.32	0.22	0.13	0.13	-0.33	0.01
22.	Communication	0.01	0.01	0.01	0.01		
23.	Services						
23a.	Education & Research	0.00	0.00	0.00	0.00		
23b.	Medical Services	0.00	0.00	0.00	0.00		
23c.	Business Services	0.00	0.07	0.00	0.14		
23d.	Personal Services	0.01	0.01	0.04	0.04		

Sources: Ministry of Labor, *Census of Wages*; Statistics Bureau, Management and
Coordination Agency, *Input-Output Tables*

TABLE III-9 (continued)
**Foreign Trade Ratio to Final Demand
and Wage Premiums**

	wage premiums (all workers)		wage premiums (HS)		wage premiums (COL)		change in wage premiums		
	1979	1994	1979	1994	1979	1994	(all) 94/79	(HS) 94/79	(COL) 94/79
1.	-0.02	-0.02	-0.02	-0.04	0.06	0.09	-0.06	0.60	0.47
2.	-0.11	-0.13	-0.12	-0.14	-0.08	-0.09	0.19	0.19	0.13
3.	-0.18	-0.25	-0.19	-0.25	-0.09	-0.11	0.37	0.36	0.19
4.	-0.12	-0.13	-0.12	-0.13	-0.09	-0.09	0.04	0.08	-0.09
5.	0.05	0.04	0.05	0.03	0.05	0.04	-0.26	-0.43	-0.15
6.	-0.06	-0.07	-0.06	-0.07	-0.05	-0.06	0.23	0.23	0.39
7.	0.06	0.00	0.06	-0.02	0.07	0.05	-1.04	-1.36	-0.36
8.	-0.02	-0.06	-0.02	-0.07	-0.01	-0.02	1.66	2.01	1.54
9.	-0.04	-0.04	-0.03	-0.03	-0.07	-0.06	0.13	0.03	-0.06
10.	-0.02	-0.03	-0.02	-0.03	-0.05	-0.05	0.32	0.38	0.09
11.	-0.09	-0.08	-0.09	-0.09	-0.06	-0.05	-0.09	-0.09	-0.24
12.	0.10	-0.02	0.11	-0.01	0.04	-0.04	-1.18	-1.08	-2.00
13.	-0.04	-0.07	-0.03	-0.07	-0.07	-0.07	0.89	1.09	-0.05
14.	-0.01	-0.01	-0.02	-0.02	0.02	0.03	-0.48	0.08	0.38
15.	0.01	0.06	0.02	0.07	-0.07	0.02	5.34	2.59	-1.32
16.	0.08	0.14	0.10	0.15	0.03	0.07	0.73	0.50	1.91
17.		0.12		0.15		0.01			
18.	-0.05	-0.08	-0.04	-0.05	-0.11	-0.13	0.67	0.23	0.15
19.	0.19	0.18	0.23	0.27	0.09	0.10	-0.05	0.17	0.15
20.	0.15	0.12	0.15	0.14	0.15	0.08	-0.22	-0.07	-0.45
21.	-0.02	-0.06	-0.01	-0.06	-0.05	-0.09	2.67	3.58	0.82
22.		0.10		0.11		0.07			
23.	0.05		0.00						
23a.		0.13		0.07		0.13			
23b.		0.17		0.13		0.19			
23c.		0.01		-0.01		0.04			
23d.		-0.04		-0.02		-0.08			

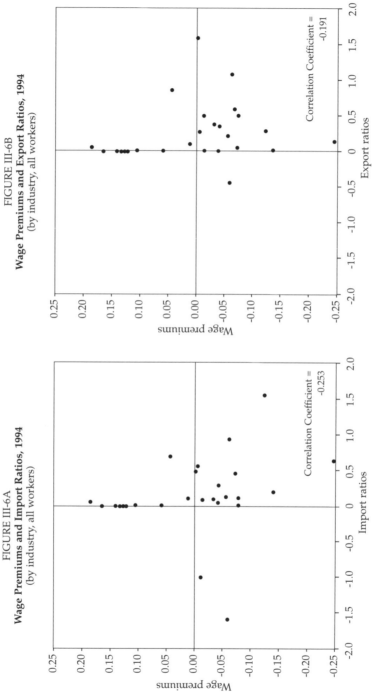

FIGURE III-6A
Wage Premiums and Import Ratios, 1994
(by industry, all workers)

Note: This figure has been plotted from Table III-9. The import ratios for 26 industries are taken from the fourth column of numbers in Table III-9. The wage premiums for 1994 for these 26 industries are taken from the eighth column in Table III-9. One striking aspect of this figure is the concentration of higher wage premiums in industries not involved in trade.

FIGURE III-6B
Wage Premiums and Export Ratios, 1994
(by industry, all workers)

Note: This figure has been plotted from Table III-9. The export ratios for 26 industries are taken from the second column of numbers in Table III-9. The wage premiums for 1994 for these 26 industries are taken from the eighth column in Table III-9. One striking aspect of this figure (as in Figure III-6A) is the concentration of higher wage premiums in industries not involved in trade.

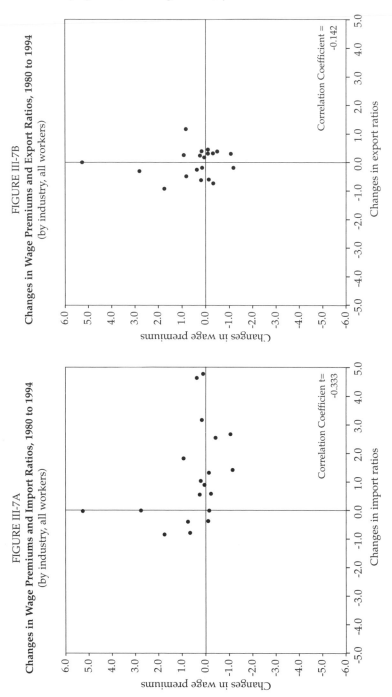

FIGURE III-7A
Changes in Wage Premiums and Import Ratios, 1980 to 1994
(by industry, all workers)

Changes in wage premiums

Changes in import ratios

Correlation Coefficient t= -0.333

Note: This figure has been plotted from Table III-9. The changes in import ratios from 1980 to 1994 are taken from the sixth column of numbers in Table III-9. The changes in wage premiums between 1979 and 1994 are taken from the thirteenth column in Table III-9.

FIGURE III-7B
Changes in Wage Premiums and Export Ratios, 1980 to 1994
(by industry, all workers)

Changes in wage premiums

Changes in export ratios

Correlation Coefficient = -0.142

Note: This figure has been plotted from Table III-9. The changes in export ratios from 1980 to 1994 are taken from the fifth column of numbers in Table III-9. The changes in wage premiums between 1979 and 1994 are taken from the thirteenth column in Table III-9.

Looking at the relationship between foreign trade and industrial premiums (Table III-9 and Figures III-6A and III-6B), one may notice that (1) the industrial premiums of the tradable goods sectors, which compete either with exports or with imports, are generally low, while (2) domestic sectors are divided into those which enjoy high industrial premiums and those whose industrial premiums are low. The correlation coefficient between export ratio and premiums in 1994 is -0.191, and that between import ratio and premiums is -0.253. Relatively low wage premiums in tradable goods sectors combined with relatively high wage premiums of some of the domestic sectors should be important to explain why internal and international prices diverge widely in Japan. However, the picture is completely different from the United States where wages in tradable goods sectors are generally high compared to the domestic sector. There does not apparently exist an industry in Japan that enjoys market power in the way that Borjas and Ramey (1993) assumed with respect to American tradable goods (consumer durable) industries. From the start, Japan lacks what is to be destroyed in their model.

Still foreign penetration into the Japanese market and the Japanese retreat from foreign markets drive wage premiums of tradable sectors further down, as is shown in Table III-9 and Figures III-7A and III-7B. Trade contributes to making the wage distribution more unequal, as it depresses the already lower wages in tradable goods sectors. As there exist other intervening factors such as those discussed above, we get the general picture of wage income as more equally distributed.

D. THE FUTURE

The same assumptions that were made in the preceding chapter for the United States (see also Lawrence [1996a], chapter 7) are adopted in drawing an extreme future scenario for Japan here. In other words, it is assumed that the low-skill-intensive manufacturing industries (basic industries) are transferred to developing countries and that Japan specializes in high-skill-intensive manufacturing industries (high-skill industries) as well as in non-manufacturing industries.

The assumptions are bold, and many objections are possible. As noted earlier, the Japanese perception is that competition is taking place not only with developing nations endowed abundantly with low-skilled labor, but also with developing nations which are rapidly catching up with advanced nations technologically. It is not safe to fix

TABLE III-10
Japanese Manufacturing Industries:
Trade and Employment Characteristics, 1990

		hs/emp	ldc exp/GDP	ldc imp/GDP	share of ldc exp	share of ldc imp	share of man emp	share of man GDP	hs/col wages
6	Chemicals	.668	.186	.061	.099	.057	.035	.077	.825
15	Precision Machines	.767	.269	.038	.034	.008	.023	.018	.764
13	Electrical Machines	.780	.274	.050	.303	.097	.170	.160	.720
16	Miscellaneous Manufact	.781	.035	.067	.038	.128	.214	.158	.767
12	General Machines	.787	.177	.015	.160	.024	.117	.131	.867
7	Oil and Coal	.813	.064	.434	.015	.179	.003	.034	
14	Transport Equipment	.835	.257	.005	.173	.006	.095	.098	.893
	Total High Skill	**.781**	**.176**	**.061**	**.823**	**.499**	**.657**	**.677**	**.797**
9+10	Basic Metals	.843	.179	.216	.097	.203	.044	.078	.893
3	Food	.861	.008	.143	.006	.179	.106	.102	.723
11	Metals	.877	.043	.015	.017	.011	.072	.059	.850
8	Ceramic, Stone & Clay	.878	.068	.046	.017	.020	.038	.036	.798
5	Pulp & Lumber	.896	.057	.056	.011	.019	.025	.028	.781
4	Textiles	.915	.200	.297	.029	.074	.057	.021	.668
	Total Basic	**.880**	**.079**	**.129**	**.177**	**.505**	**.343**	**.323**	**.764**
	Total	**.827**	**.145**	**.083**	**1.00**	**1.00**	**1.00**	**1.00**	**.770**

Sources: Ministry of Labor, *Basic Survey on Wage Structure;* Economic Planning Agency, *Annual Report on National Accounts;* OECD, *Foreign Trade by Commodities*

Notes: hs/emp = share of full-time employment with high school degree or less in 1990 (enterprises with more than five persons); ldc exp = Japanese exports of manufactured goods to developing countries (developing countries = all countries except OECD countries minus Spain, Portugal and Turkey); ldc imp = Japanese imports of manufactured goods from developing countries; man emp = employment in manufacturing; Basic Metals = iron and steel + nonferrous metals; wages = average monthly contractual cash earnings (enterprises with more than 10 employees, without part-timers).

the boundaries between skill-rich and skill-poor countries because innovations in technology, human capital accumulation, and capital mobility are rapidly changing the location of industries all over the world. Competition is also taking place in non-manufacturing industries. Still the exercise is worthwhile for the sake of guesswork and of comparison.

Based on the comparison between Table II-4 for U.S. manufacturing industries and Table III-10 constructed in a similar manner for Japanese manufacturing industries, we can make the following observations: (1) The ratios of high school graduates among manufacturing workers is generally higher in Japan than in the United States. (2) Differences in the ratios by industry are smaller in Japan. There does not exist such a wide discontinuity between high-skill industries and basic industries as exists in the United States. (3) The rank order of the ratios of high school graduates by industry coincides in both countries, however.

It is not as easy to distinguish high-skilled from basic industries in Japan as in the United States. We draw a line of demarcation in Table III-10 at a ratio of high school graduates of 84 percent (in contrast with about 60 percent in Table II-4 for the United States) with some degree of arbitrariness, also taking the classification in the United States into consideration.[11] The result in Table III-10 is a somewhat larger share of high-skilled industries in output and employment (68 percent and 66 percent in Japan in contrast with 57 percent and 54 percent in Table II-4 for the United States). The ratios of imports from developing countries in high-skill and basic industries in Japan are 6 percent and 13 percent respectively, while those in Table II-4 for the United States are 8 percent and 15 percent.

The distinction between the two types of industries is not so clear-cut in Japan, and this might make the reading of our scenario more ambiguous. Still, following the assumptions made in constructing the scenario for the United States in the preceding chapter (that basic industries will stop production at home, that high-skill industries will expand to offset the loss of domestic production of basic industries, and that employment coefficients in both types of industries will remain unchanged), one can infer that there will be a loss of 4.7 million jobs in basic industries, which will be compensated for by a

---

[11]Treatment of the transportation equipment industry may be somewhat problematic. Table III-10 classifies it in the group of high-skill industries in Japan, as is the case in Table II-4 for the United States. The importance of the automobile industry is common to both countries, but product-mixes other than automobiles may differ to some extent.

TABLE III-11
Future Scenario: Japan

	High-Skill Mnfctrg	Basic Mnfctrg	All Mnfctrg	Non-Mnfctrg	Japan Ecnmy
1991 Actual					
(1) GDP (¥billions)	82,011	39,208	121,219	308,642	429,860
(2) Employment (millions)	9.09	4.73	13.82	37.67	51.49
(3) GDP/Emp (1)/(2)	9,027	8,282	8,772		
(4) High School Emp (millions)	7.10	4.17	11.26	26.24	37.50
(5) College Emp (millions)	1.99	0.57	2.55	11.44	13.99
(6) HS/Emp (4)/(2)	0.78	0.88	0.82	0.70	0.73
(7) HS/COL (4)/(5)	3.57	7.33	4.41	2.29	2.68
Hypothetical					
(8) GDP	121,219	0.00	121,219	308,642	429,860
(9) Employment (8)/(3)	13.43	0.00	13.43	37.67	51.10
(10) High School Emp (6)*(9)	10.49	0.00	10.49	26.24	36.73
(11) College Emp (9)-(10)	2.94	0.00	2.94	11.44	14.37
(12) HS/COL (10)/(11)	3.57		3.57	2.29	2.56
Hypothetical - Actual					
(13) Employment (9)-(2)	+4.34	-4.73	-0.39	0.00	-0.39
(14) High School Emp (10)-(4)	+3.39	-4.17	-0.77	0.00	-0.77
(15) College Emp (11)-(5)	+0.95	-0.57	+0.38	0.00	+0.38
(16) HS/COL (14)/(15)	3.57		-2.03		-2.03

Sources: Ministry of Labor, *Basic Survey on Wage Structure*; Economic Planning Agency, *Annual Report on National Accounts*

gain of 4.3 million jobs in high-skill industries. The net loss of manufacturing jobs due to the change in industrial structure will be 0.4 million or 3 percent and 0.75 percent of manufacturing and total employment. The shift also affects employment of high school and college graduates differently. The manufacturing jobs for college graduates will expand by 0.4 million, or 15 percent, while those for high school graduates will diminish by 0.8 million, or 7 percent.

Again, objections to the procedure are possible. By expanding foreign trade, Japan can import low-skill-intensive goods less expensively than those produced at home and export high-skill-intensive goods under more favorable conditions. In other words, gains from trade must be taken into consideration. On the other hand, the scenario shows the need for the changed demand for labor (as a whole and for college and high school graduates respectively) to be somehow balanced through wage adjustment, human capital formation, and shifts in the industrial structure. No one can be sure how costly the process of transformation will be as long as exact values of several elasticities (such as substitution between skilled and less-skilled labor) are not known. Needless to say, productivity will not be the same in the future as it is today. Still, the exercise suggests that the adjustment needed for globalization of markets is within the scope of advanced nations' capacity to adjust.

E. CONCLUDING REMARKS:
MORE FLEXIBLE LABOR MARKETS NEEDED
IN A MORE INTEGRATED WORLD

In spite of our observation that foreign trade adversely affected employment of less-educated workers as well as wage premiums of tradable goods sectors, neither unemployment nor wage inequality has emerged conspicuously so far in Japan. Surprisingly, wage differentials between college and high-school graduates, between non-production and production workers, and so on appear to have narrowed in Japan in the 1990s.

Still, the need for industrial adjustment in order to live in a more integrated world is keenly felt by the public, particularly in connection with the prolonged recession in recent years and with the persistent high cost structure of the domestic economy. Flexibility in labor markets is called for in order for restructuring to be achieved. It is true that the life-time employment system helps to keep unemployment from exploding for the time being. However, it has delayed adjustment and prolonged stagnation. Faced with slow growth of the economy and an aging workforce, firms are forced to restrain the increase of wage bills and are trying to amend seniority wages. This move, somewhat paradoxically, brought about narrower wage inequality.

In addition to policies discussed in other chapters, a special emphasis should be put on the need for reforms in labor market practices that will facilitate more flexible industrial adjustment in an age of globalization, particularly in the case of Japan.

IV. EUROPE

A. TRADE FLOWS WITH
THE NON-OECD AREA

There is no obvious a priori reason for thinking that trade with low-cost countries should be regarded as a major threat to the satisfactory economic performance of the European economies. Trade flows with the non-OECD area have expanded steadily, broadly in step with trade inside the OECD area as a whole, but more slowly than intra-European trade, over at least the last three decades. Trade with the non-OECD area has been approximately balanced for the European countries as a whole.

In manufactured products, which are the focus of the present study, Europe has tended to run a sizeable surplus throughout the period, though with a declining trend; the surplus peaked at more than 3 percent of European GDP, but it has recently approached 1 percent of GDP. This is a smaller surplus than Japan's, but a more comfortable position than North America's stable, small deficit. These modest departures from balanced trade in manufactures have to some extent their counterparts in the very different degrees of dependence on imports of energy and other primary products in the three Trilateral regions, Japan being by far the most dependent on imports of such products, North America the least (Table IV-1).

If one examines in more detail the trade flows in manufactured products of the member states of the European Union and of some of the larger EU countries in particular, the impression of steady, well-balanced trade flows is confirmed. The modest share of the non-OECD countries in EU imports from non-European countries has moved up, but very gradually and largely in parallel in the four largest EU countries (Germany, France, Italy, and the United Kingdom), in all cases primarily as a result of greater market penetration by the successful Asian economies (China, the four Asian Tigers and the ASEAN countries). But the share of the low-cost producers in the total market for manufactured products remains

TABLE IV-1
Developing Country Import Penetration
(as percentage of apparent consumption)

	European Union			North America			Japan		
	1980/81	1985/86	1990/91	1980/81	1985/86	1990/91	1980/81	1985/86	1990/91
All commodities	7.57	5.55	4.24	5.11	4.29	5.29	7.90	4.67	4.03
Primary products	30.11	20.72	16.88	22.33	10.66	13.05	48.19	34.33	30.61
Manufactures	2.74	2.78	2.69	2.31	3.42	4.32	1.69	1.43	1.97
Textiles and fibres	4.95	4.33	4.84	2.08	3.26	3.80	2.04	1.92	2.63
Clothing, footwear and travel goods	14.24	16.14	19.56	14.35	24.83	29.70	6.84	8.86	12.21
Wood products, paper and printing	1.74	1.49	1.50	0.78	1.23	1.39	0.81	0.78	1.62
Chemicals	1.59	1.61	1.31	0.76	1.12	1.19	0.86	1.06	1.11
Transport equipment	1.10	0.84	0.92	0.34	0.79	1.87	0.20	0.09	0.14
Machinery and other manufactures	2.49	3.30	3.99	3.48	6.23	8.86	0.86	0.88	1.74

Source: UNCTAD, *Handbook of International Trade and Development Statistics, 1987* (Supplement) and 1993, New York

small and clearly smaller than that observed in the North American market (Table IV-1). Neither the past experience nor the present position qualifies as alarmingly fast penetration of European markets by low-cost producers.

As already noted, European exports of manufactures to the non-OECD countries continue to exceed imports, but by a shrinking margin. Given the very rapid economic growth in the Asian economies in particular, one would have expected the share of EU exports which go to them to have risen, but that has not been the case. The Europeans have apparently been less successful than the North Americans and the Japanese in reaping the benefits of the dynamism of the Asian economies, though this observation could presumably to some extent be explained by geography. The evolution is roughly parallel for the four largest EU countries on the export side over the past 10-15 years, though the importance of markets outside the OECD area differs somewhat between them; these markets are more important for France, which has the largest surplus in trade in manufactured products, followed by Italy.

To get a better picture of the challenges and opportunities of trading with the low-cost producers it is useful to disaggregate at a minimum to the 2-digit level (of the Standard International Trade Classification of manufactures) and to rank the industries according to the degree of market penetration. The average market share of the low-cost producers for all of manufacturing industry in the EU has recently crept over 5 percent—an increase of two percentage points over the most recent decade—but in some sectors penetration has moved much higher (Table IV-2). For five industries it is more than twice the average figure, but only in one—"other industries," covering largely toys, jewelry and musical instruments—has the market share of the low-cost producers become dominant. The capture of market shares has also been impressive in leather goods, office machinery, clothing and footwear, and textiles. The list in Table IV-2 does not suggest that the advances made by the low-cost producers are only, or even primarily, in low-technology industries.

If one looks at the other side of the trade flows in manufactured products, the average share of EU countries' exports destined for the low-cost producers is around 7 percent, roughly unchanged over the recent decade. The importance of these markets to EU exporters is the greatest for machinery and parts, transport equipment (excluding autos) and leather goods, but textiles and

TABLE IV-2
**Share of Non-OECD Exporters in the
Demand in EU Markets for Manufactures**
(percentage)

SITC		1992	1992-1982
49	Other industries (toys, jewelry, musical instruments)	80.7	47.6
44	Leather goods	29.0	11.3
45	Clothing and footwear	25.8	10.2
43	Textiles	15.0	6.4
33	Office machinery, IT equipment	12.8	11.1
37	Precision and optical instruments	8.4	4.0
22	Iron and steel	7.9	1.9
46	Wood and furniture	7.1	0.4
36	Transportation equipment (excl. autos)	6.3	4.4
34	Electricity, electronic products	6.0	3.6
Average for all manufacturing industries		**5.2**	**1.9**

Source: Buigues and Jacquemin (1995), p. 70

artificial fibers are also—somewhat surprisingly—found in the category where the importance of the export markets outside the OECD area is greater than average.

This summary record of trade flows permits a simple classification of the eighteen 2-digit industries (Table IV-3). This table shows that seven sectors of manufacturing industry exhibit important two-way

TABLE IV-3
Non-OECD Area Shares of EU Exports and Demand, by Industry

Share of EU demand met by exports from non-OECD area

		low	high
Share of EU exports going to non-OECD area	low	non-metallic mineral manufactures manufactures of metal automobiles beverages and tobacco paper and newsprint rubber products	office machinery, IT equipment footwear and apparel wood and wood manufactures
	high	artificial fibres machinery and parts	iron and steel electrical and electronic products transport equipment (excl. autos) precision and optical instruments textiles leather goods other industries (toys, jewelry, musical instruments)

Source: Buigues and Jacquemin (1995), p. 71

trade (iron and steel, electricity and electronic products, transport equipment [excluding autos], precision and optical instruments, textiles, leather goods, and other industries) while six other sectors are characterized by only limited trade between the EU countries and the low-cost producers.

It is possible that the impression left by this analysis, viz., that exchange of similar manufactured products (or intra-industry trade) has become important, is misleading. The classification of industrial sectors may be so rough as to conceal that the products exchanged within sectors are in fact quite different and hence indicative of a high degree of specialization within each industrial sector. If one looks, for example, at electrical and electronic products, EU exports consist to an important extent of telecommunications equipment and electrical investment goods, while domestic household appliances are important components of exports of low-cost producers to the EU. Furthermore, textiles is not a homogeneous category; the EU countries export primarily relatively sophisticated goods in a higher price range than they import. The impression that intra-industry trade has become highly significant therefore has to be studied at a more disaggregated level. The issue is important because, as was argued in Chapter I, the adjustment to growth in intra-industry trade flows is supposed to be less onerous than in the case of inter-industry trade, where whole industries may disappear under the pressure of competition with low-cost producers.

Buigues and Jacquemin (1995) have carried the analysis of the importance of intra-industry trade between the European Union and the non-OECD area further by looking at the 110 subsectors which comprise the 3-digit classification of manufacturing industries. They compare traditional indicators of intra-industry trade flows with other industrial countries to those with the non-OECD area. They find that for both groups of trade flows the share of intra-industry trade has risen since the early 1980s, but that intra-industry flows constitute a smaller share of trade with the non-OECD area than with other industrial countries (just less than 50 percent as against 75 percent) in the early 1990s. The gap between the two appears to be narrowing over time, suggesting that the nature of European trade is becoming more similar, regardless of who the trading partner is. Again, the four largest EU countries exhibit similar trends, but slightly different levels of intra-industry trade; Italy, followed closely by the United Kingdom, has a somewhat higher share of such trade than Germany and France.

The data for disaggregated flows of trade in manufactured products may be studied further by trying to explain which factors appear to have influenced the penetration of exports from low-cost producers in EU markets. The explanatory factors used are those suggested by trade theory. Three factors appear to have been significant: the stock of capital per worker, the qualifications of the labor force (measured by the share of white-collar employees in an industry) and economies of scale, represented simply by the number of employees per firm. The higher any of these factors, the lower the expected degree of market penetration by the low-cost producers. On the whole, effects in this direction are found in studies by the OECD (1994) and Buigues and Jacquemin (1995), with some interesting variations among EU countries. The qualifications of the labor force seem particularly important in explaining German trade patterns, while larger average size of firms is very important in France and the United Kingdom. These linkages seem plausible, although they cannot be regarded as firmly established; they suggest the types of market-oriented defenses which can help to make European manufacturing industry retain its competitiveness vis-à-vis low-cost producers.

B. EUROPEAN UNEMPLOYMENT

Why then is there such concern in the European public debate about competition in an increasingly globalized economy? The explanation is found in the combination of the alarming rise in the average rate of unemployment in nearly all European countries over the past 20-25 years and rigidities in the wage structure which have tended to impart a stronger upward trend to unemployment among the less-skilled. Figures IV-1 and IV-2 summarize the main differences vis-à-vis the United States.

In the United States, as noted in Chapter II, employment creation has continued at a rapid pace throughout the past 20-25 years, only temporarily checked by the two recessions following the oil price shocks of 1973-4 and 1979-80 and the recession of the early 1990s, while average real wages have moved up very slowly. In the European Community—Figure IV-1 refers to the 12 member states prior to the 1995 enlargement but the picture would not have been significantly different had the three most recent entrants been included—real wages per employee have risen by more than half, while employment has increased very slowly and primarily in the

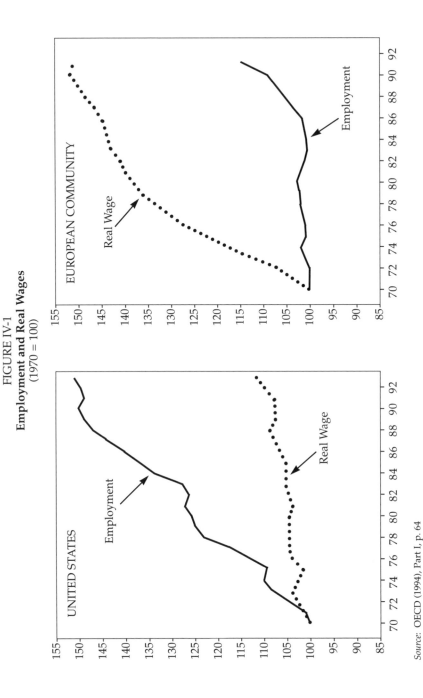

FIGURE IV-1
Employment and Real Wages
(1970 = 100)

Source: OECD (1994), Part I, p. 64

Note: Real wages are total compensation per employee deflated by the GDP deflator.

public sector. In the aggregate Europe offers a mirror image of the United States, suggesting a strong trade-off between employment and real wages. This sharp contrast in experience has been studied intensively by the international organizations, notably in the massive OECD *Jobs Study* of 1994 and in recent reports by the ILO (1995) and the World Bank (1995), and it has provided the agenda for two special G-7 meetings of Ministers of Finance, Trade and Labor in Detroit in 1994 and in Lille in 1996. Presentations by Bergsten, Ferrer and Nukazawa to the 1994 annual meeting of the Trilateral Commission already analyzed these major differences, noting also—in a way foreshadowing the more detailed analysis of Japan in Chapter III above—that the apparent escape of Japan from both rising unemployment and non-stagnant real wages requires some important qualifications (see Bergsten et al [1994]).

The contrast between Trilateral regions with respect to growing inequalities could hardly be more striking as well, as shown in Figure IV-2. Since 1980 an often-used measure of income inequality—the ratio of the upper ten percent in the earnings distribution to the bottom ten percent—has risen sharply in North America, though not quite as fast as in the United Kingdom, while most Continental Europe countries (with France and Germany among them) have experienced stable or even shrinking wage differentials. Japan is an intermediate case, showing a modest rise in earnings inequality to 1990, though, as argued in Chapter III, this tendency appears to have been reversed in recent years.

The reasons for the greater rigidity in the Continental European wage structure are not easy to pinpoint. They do not appear to be primarily due to a higher degree of unionization, although a number of European countries have a higher degree of unionization than the Unites States and centralized, or at least sectoral, wage bargaining. Unionization rates have been falling in Europe and some countries with particularly rigid wage structures, notably France, have a low degree of union membership, though that appears to be compensated by the tendency to extend to non-unionized labor the wage agreements made with unions. There is some evidence that legislated or collectively agreed minimum wages have contributed to making the wage structure less flexible, and that high unemployment benefit entitlements (particularly when benefit administration has not been kept so tight as to minimize disincentives to seek work) have provided payments for the less-skilled still in the work force at higher levels than would be consistent

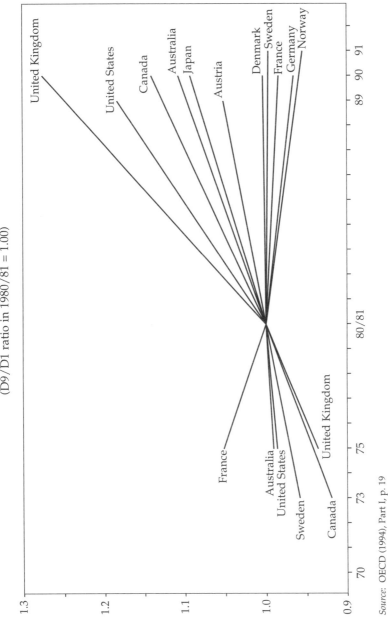

FIGURE IV-2
Trends in Earning Distributions
(D9/D1 ratio in 1980/81 = 1.00)

Source: OECD (1994), Part I, p. 19

Note: The measure of earnings distribution is the ratio of the lower limit of earnings received by the top 10 percent (9th decile) of all male workers (both sexes for Denmark and Norway) relative to the upper limit of earnings received by the bottom 10 percent (1st decile).

with the balance between supply and demand.

Whatever the explanation there has been a clearly observable tendency for unemployment rates among the less-skilled to rise relative to those for the skilled. In France, Germany and Italy unemployment rates for men between age 25 and 64 with lower secondary education or less have more than doubled over the most recent decade for which observations are available, while the rate for those with upper secondary education or more has increased much less. For women there is a similar though less marked tendency for educational levels to widen the differentials in employment trends, but the level of unemployment is much higher for women. The ratio between unemployment percentages for less-skilled and skilled workers, using educational attainment as a basis for classification, is not universally higher in countries with a more rigid wage structure, but it has moved up significantly over the past 10-15 years in these countries, while it has remained more stable in the Anglo-Saxon countries and in Japan.

Another important feature of the European unemployment problem is its differential impact on the young, i.e., under 25 years of age. During the economic upturn in the second half of the 1980s youth unemployment actually fell relative to that of older members of the work force, although it remained more than twice the rate for older workers even at its trough in 1990 (16 percent as against 7 percent). But this trend was reversed in the recession of the early 1990s; hence the OECD *Jobs Study* of 1994 could not take the worsening fully into account. In 1994 youth unemployment reached 22 percent—again more than twice the rate for older workers. In some countries it was much higher (Spain 45 percent, Italy 32 percent, France 29 percent), as indicated in Table IV-4. Only Germany and two smaller EU countries (Denmark and the Netherlands) appear to have escaped the general trend for youth unemployment to stabilize around twice the average rate. The average EU unemployment rate has been fluctuating around 11 percent in 1994-95 and the slowdown in 1995-96 has regenerated fears that a reduction in the rate is unlikely to be major and sustained.

High unemployment with a particularly vicious incidence among the less-skilled and the young is an alarming phenomenon which can prove even more socially divisive than growing wage differentials between the less-skilled and the skilled. At the same time there is little readiness in most EU countries to consider the remedies accepted in U.S.-style labor markets for checking growing average

TABLE IV-4
Unemployment Features in European Union Countries, 1994

	Unemployment Rate (%)	Youth Unemployment Rate (%)	Long-Term Unemployment[2]	Low-Skilled Unemployment[3]
			(% share of total unemployment)	
Belgium	10.0	24.1	58	52
Denmark	8.2	10.7	32	31
France	12.3	29.1	38	46
Germany	8.4	8.6	44	22
Greece	8.9	27.7	51	40
Ireland	14.7	23.3	59[1]	64
Italy	11.4	32.3	62	59
Luxembourg	3.5	7.7	30	63
Netherlands	7.0	10.7	49	32
Portugal	7.0	15.1	43	79
Spain	24.3	45.3	53	68
United Kingdom	9.6	17.0	45	58
Austria				
Finland	18.4	33.6	21	
Sweden	9.8	22.6	10[1]	
European Union	**11.2**	**21.8**	**48**	**50**

Source: European Commission Annual Report 1996, Brussels, p. 23

[1] 1993
[2] Unemployed for more than 12 months
[3] Educational level lower than upper secondary; share calculated for persons aged 15 to 59 years.

unemployment and the tendency to affect the job opportunities of the weakest most strongly. Simply allowing wage differentials to widen in order to price the less-skilled—and the young—into jobs squeezed out by a relative fall in the demand for them relative to supply is not considered socially acceptable. Such developments would appear to conflict with the notion of assuring a certain minimum standard of consumption possibilities at the lower end of the income scale, whether through minimum wage or unemployment benefit levels which set a floor to pay for those who actually work. The search for "a third way" between wage flexibility (which seems to imply that there will be many "working poor") and the present Continental European protective system for the low-paid is much talked about—for instance by President Chirac at the April 1996 Lille G-7 employment conference—but is only at an early and highly tentative stage. Most uncontroversial measures that can be thought of, in particular upgrading of the work force with special emphasis on the less-skilled and the young, are likely to work very slowly.

In this climate there is a search for quicker remedies and it is well-recognized that the precarious present state of public finances and their likely deterioration due to demographic factors early in the next century leave little scope for any macroeconomic stimulation of a traditional type. Furthermore, the EU countries have signed on to the convergence criteria of the Maastricht Treaty which put the main emphasis on budgetary consolidation and monetary policies oriented towards price stability. Finally, the framework of the Single European Market puts severe limits on the extent to which they can use national measures of industrial policies individually to foster the growth of jobs in their respective industries.

It is therefore logical in political terms that the EU countries are presently looking at the various instruments that still seem to be available, even though their use would be dangerous to the welfare of Europe collectively. One such instrument is the exchange rate; another is a slowdown in the process of globalization before it accelerates further through some form of EU preferential arrangement.

As far as the exchange rate is concerned, there is little doubt that the countries in Europe which have maintained stable exchange rates among themselves throughout nearly a decade share a perception that they have suffered an important loss in competitiveness vis-à-vis their other trading partners—the United States, the rapidly growing economies in Asia with currencies largely linked to the dollar, and, most importantly, those EU countries which gave up their linkage to the strongest European currencies in 1992 and allowed their exchange rates to weaken very significantly. Hence the European strong-currency countries are looking on the one hand for tight arrangements with those EU member states which are unlikely for one reason or another to join them when—or if—they succeed in a couple of years to make the decision to embark on a full-scale monetary union with a single currency, and on the other hand for a strengthening of important non-EU currencies vis-à-vis their own. Both of these efforts currently seem likely to end in frustration; the likely non-participants in monetary union seem either uninterested in, or see themselves as incapable of, entering into any formal commitments to maintain stable exchange rates with the strong EU currencies, while the depreciation of the latter vis-à-vis major third currencies, notably the dollar, is a highly uncertain prospect.

In a climate of historically high unemployment which has affected the weaker parts of the work force differentially, with domestic macroeconomic instruments on a pre-set course and a perception of weakened competitiveness in part through currency appreciation which cannot realistically be reversed or even prevented from going further, frustrated policymakers and participants in the European public debate are tempted to look at steps that could protect them more efficiently against an ominous process of globalization which is seen to continue to erode the scope for private sector job creation at home. The expansion of trade with neighboring countries in Central and Eastern Europe (which look like they will become major low-cost competitors) has added to this perception, indicated in diminishing popular support for EU enlargement.

C. EFFECTS OF TRADE ON UNEMPLOYMENT

The above discussion of the importance of trade flows already strongly suggests that slowing down trade integration with low-cost producers is unlikely to become an important remedy for the strains in European labor markets. Trade flows in manufactured products have so far been modest and appoximately balanced or in surplus. Trade is beginning to look more rather than less like the intra-industry trade which dominates inside the EU and in Europe's trade with the other Trilateral regions, although it remains qualitatively different. To the extent that the past is any guide to future problems, trade flows between the EU and the non-OECD area should enhance rather than diminish overall welfare.

There are few studies available which focus directly on the linkage of trade flows with low-cost producers to employment in Europe and which do so on a comparable basis for a number of countries in Europe. What is available is not necessarily reliable, partly because the material refers to periods ending several years ago, and partly because the studies may contain a downward bias (since they rely on industry averages for the use of labor rather than on jobs lost in the firms which have been reducing employment or have been eliminated outright). We have looked at two studies which are both products of the OECD *Jobs Study.*

One study analyzes the overall impact on employment in manufacturing and compares the effects of trade inside the OECD area to those of trade with non-OECD countries for different periods prior to the mid-1980s (Table IV-5). The sample consists of the three largest EU economies and compares them to the United States and Japan.

All three European countries as well as the United States have lost jobs in manufacturing industries on a moderate scale when the net factor content of labor in total trade flows is calculated by using an input-output table for a year in the mid-1980s. But the explanation for this loss of jobs varies widely. France had the most favorable experience in trade with non-OECD countries—actually a small gain in employment. This observation, which is more optimistic than a more recent study of the 1977-93 period by Cortes, Jean and Pisani-Ferry (1995), makes it somewhat surprising that the claims for slowing down globalization have arisen with particular strength in France. Germany had a loss corresponding to roughly 2 percent of total employment, but this was largely compensated for by gains from trade with other OECD countries; it should be noted that the period 1978-86 was one in which German competitiveness was generally strong because of an over-appreciated U.S. dollar and low German inflation relative to that of European trading partners. The United Kingdom also experienced job losses corresponding to about 2 percent of total employment, but the loss due to intra-OECD trade was much larger than that attributable to trade with the non-OECD area; the first half of the 1980s was a period when sterling was overvalued. Japan is the only G-5 country to come out with employment gains from trade with both groups of countries. The United States lost jobs due to both kinds of trade, but the loss was less than 5 percent of the 23 million jobs created in the U.S. economy in the 1972-85 period.

As already hinted at in Chapter I, there are reasons to believe that the net factor content of trade underestimates actual job losses because it fails to take into account the vulnerability of particularly labor-intensive forms of production in any given industrial sector.

TABLE IV-5
Effects of Trade on Employment in Selected OECD Countries
(various periods, thousands)

	France	Germany	United Kingdom	United States	Japan
	1972-85	1978-86	1968-84	1972-85	1972-85
All trade in manufactures	-233	-47	-2,333	-1,645	+5,300
Trade among OECD partners	-370	+409	-1,833	-611	+4,074
Trade with non-OECD countries	+137	-456	-500	-1,034	+1,226
as % of total employment[1]	≈0	-1.7%	-2.1%	-1.0%	+2.0%
Memo item: Overall change in employment[2]	+97	+726	-785	+23,175	+6,607

Source: Derived from Table 3.10 of the OECD *Jobs Study*, Part I (OECD, 1994)

[1] total employment in the most recent year of the period for the country in question
[2] includes employment in non-manufacturing sectors

The firms which scale down operations or disappear as a result of low-cost competition are likely to be in that category. There is unfortunately no reliable way of assessing the importance of this bias, which is also noted in Chapter II on the United States. Preliminary work for a study by the Ministry of Industry in Denmark of job losses due to trade with the non-OECD area suggests that taking into account intra-firm differences in labor intensity in the production of a number of industrial sectors may lead to an upward correction of the estimates based on industry averages of typically 20-40 percent—a significant revision, but not to a different order of magnitude as suggested notably by Wood (1994).

The other study disaggregates manufacturing industry in 12 OECD countries (and 8 EU countries separately). It looks at selected industries and at industrial groupings labelled "low-manual," "medium-manual" and "high-manual" (Table IV-6). This study of Larre (1995) finds a significant negative association between the change in relative employment and relative import penetration by non-OECD countries for a small number of manufacturing industries in 12 OECD countries (textiles, apparel and leather; office and computing machinery; and radio and TV communications) and 8 EU countries (office and computing machinery). But when groups of industries are studied, the impact is modest and much smaller than for global import penetration, reflecting the small share of the total trade with non-OECD countries. The influence of trade with low-cost producers is clearer, somewhat surprisingly, in the low- and medium-manual groupings. This runs counter to the widespread notion that the loss of jobs is most important in industries which use less-skilled labor relatively intensively (high-manual). This tentative conclusion underlies the view presented more fully in Chapter III on Japan, viz., that the challenge from new trading partners arises also outside the industries that use less-skilled labor intensively.

In short, there is little evidence that competition from low-cost producers has historically produced job losses on a major scale in Europe's manufacturing industry, or that the losses that have been observed are concentrated in the sectors which employ primarily less-skilled workers. As in the case of the United States, the trade flows with the non-OECD area have simply been too small—and a fortiori since the U.S. trade with these countries is larger than Europe's—to attribute to them an important part of the responsibility for the rise in Europe's average unemployment rate or the relative deterioration in job opportunities for the less-skilled.

The rigidity of wage structures in most European countries will in one sense have magnified the adjustment problem relative to that facing the United States with its much more flexible wages. As Krugman (1995) has argued, the job losses estimated by means of the net factor content method fail to take account of the multiplier effect of the rise in unemployment due to the failure of wages to adjust. In other words the decline in employment opportunities for the less-skilled becomes greater than the net quantity of such labor embodied in the trade flows. Krugman's subsequent calculation of the changes in relative wages (and prices) required to remove these magnifying effects in the European economies suggest that only modest changes in relative wages and prices would have been sufficient, hence providing a rationale for the finding of Lawrence and others that relative prices of products with a high content of less-skilled labor have not fallen by much in the flexible-wage economy of the United States.

TABLE IV-6
Relative Employment and Trade with the Non-OECD Area
(changes over three time periods)

	Import penetration from:		Export intensity towards:	
	World	Non-OECD (excl. OPEC)	World	Non-OECD (excl. OPEC)

12 OECD Countries

Industry Groupings

low-manual	-0.08**	-0.03**	-0.05**	-0.03**
medium-manual	-0.11*	-0.04*	0.0	0.0
high-manual	-0.19**	-0.01	-0.06**	-0.01

Selected Industries[†]

textiles, apparel, leather	-0.02	-0.16*		
wood products and furniture			-0.06	-0.14*
iron and steel			+0.12	+0.10**
office and computing machinery	-0.21*	-0.19**	-0.21*	-0.09
radio and TV communications	-0.77**	-0.14**		
other transport equipment[††]			-0.06*	-0.05**

8 European Countries

Industry Groupings

low-manual	-0.15*	-0.03**	+0.01	-0.01
medium-manual	-0.14*	-0.04	+0.02	-0.02
high-manual	-0.23**	0.0	-0.10*	-0.02

Selected Industries[†]

textiles, apparel, leather	+0.09	+0.29*		
wood products and furniture			-0.11	-0.20**
petroleum products			+0.14	+0.06*
non-electrical machinery			-0.38	-0.31*
office and computing machinery	+0.27	-0.24**	-0.38	-0.31*
other transport equipment[††]			+0.06	-0.03**

Source: Larre (1995), p. 27, using estimates based on the OECD/DSTI STAN database

Note: The coefficients express the changes in the ratio of employment in the industry or industry group relative to total manufacturing employment which can be statistically associated with a one percent change in the ratio, relative to output, of imports from all trading partners (first column), imports from non-OECD countries (second column), global exports (third column) or exports to non-OECD countries (fourth column).

† industries with coefficients significantly different than zero.

†† other than shipbuilding, motor vehicles and aircraft industries

* coefficients significantly different from zero at the 5 percent level

** coefficients significantly different from zero at the 1 percent level

D. CONCLUSIONS

The remedies for Europe's unemployment problem and for the growing inequalities in job opportunities for the less-skilled do not lie in restraints on participation in further trade integration with the non-OECD countries. A moderate degree of wage flexibility would help to contain the problem. But the main approach has to be directed at the overwhelming part of the European economies which is not trading with new low-cost competitors and hence is only indirectly exposed to the forces of change. The public sectors in Europe are generally oversized and cannot be relied upon to provide additional job opportunities at the rate they did over much of the 1970s and 1980s. But there is major scope in the private service sector for increasing employment in Europe—provided relative wages do not preclude such growth. As a result of the relatively high wages of the less-skilled, Europe has gradually become under-supplied with private services relative to the United States and Japan. Total employment in services in Germany—a representative example of rigid wages in Europe—in 1993 stood at 258 per 1000 inhabitants compared to 302 in Japan and 339 in the United States. A major part of that "shortfall" is in personal services, but Germany also had fewer people employed in business-related services such as the financial sector and accounting. The potential for creating additional jobs in the service sector is clearly very considerable, particularly relative to the jobs at risk in trading with new partners in the global economy. Employment in the service sector (where productivity growth is typically relatively weak) has been undermined by the rise in labor costs driven by other sectors, so a decline in relative wages is a prerequisite for exploiting these employment opportunities; this is particularly the case for personal services which use much less-skilled labor and where the high rate of taxation in most European countries has driven a major wedge between the costs to the employer and take-home pay for the employed. European countries would do better by looking critically at these features of their labor markets rather than at the perceived shorter-term gains from limiting trade with and foreign direct investment in the non-OECD countries.

V. Conclusions and Policy Implications

Our survey has revealed similarities and differences among Trilateral countries. Throughout the Trilateral countries there is concern about labor market performance and the role of globalization. It is striking that there are also noteworthy contrasts in labor market performance and patterns of trade with developing countries. This diversity of experience suggests strongly that there are differences in the shocks affecting these economies and/or that domestic institutions play an important role in shaping the impact which these shocks have.

- The United States has experienced growing wage inequality (particularly in the 1980s) and sustained slow growth in average wages, but relatively low rates of unemployment. Indeed, the United States is presently at virtually full employment. America's trade patterns with developing countries are highly differentiated along lines of skill and education, i.e. American exports to developed economies are concentrated in industries which employ more highly educated workers, and the United States has experienced a growing trade deficit in manufactured goods with developing countries since the early 1980s. By contrast, American imports from developed countries are more concentrated in industries such as automobiles and steel in which workers earn premium wages.

- In Japan, particularly recently, there has been no significant trend towards widening income inequalities. If anything there has been in recent years a slight tendency towards increasing equality accompanied by considerable disguised unemployment and rising average wages. The Japanese are also concerned about international competition, but the concern reflects the problem of being squeezed out of manufacturing activities that are increasingly undertaken by the DAEs and the difficulties of moving into the industries of the future. Unlike the United States where premium wages are to be found in the highly concentrated manufacturing industries, in Japan these premiums are to be found in sectors sheltered from international trade, such as utilities. Japan's trade with developing countries is less distinctly differentiated along the lines of skill than the United States. As a result, an expansion in trade with developing countries has relatively weaker effects on wage inequality than is the case in the United States. However, since on-the-job training accounts for a much higher proportion of skills acquisition in Japan than in the United States, occupational categories appear to reflect differences more sharply than those based on educational attainment.

- In Europe the concerns relate to high rates of unemployment particularly among workers with little skill or education. There is by contrast little evidence of increasing inequality—with the exception of the United Kingdom—or of a failure of average wages to grow. Europe's trade with the developing countries is relatively small and exports of manufactures exceed imports, albeit by a shrinking margin.

Despite these differences, the overall role played by trade with developing countries seems to have been relatively small in all Trilateral countries.

We are aware of the sensitivity of this conclusion to the analytical methods used, which, though defensible, may contain a downward bias. Calculating the net factor content of trade by means of the average use of less-skilled labor may impart such a bias, since the firms initially affected by competition from low-cost competitors are likely to use more less-skilled labor than the average firm in the industry affected. Corrections for this may increase by up to half the estimate which we, like most other studies, find as the most plausible effect from trade, viz. 10-20 per cent of the observed deterioration in the indicators of relative deterioration in the position of the less-skilled in North America and in Europe.

Would the conclusion be greatly changed if one tries to look ahead as major new actors with very large populations and even lower cost levels enter the global trading system? We regard this as unlikely, though the difficulties of assessing the future challenges suggest that a high degree of confidence in asserting this would be inappropriate. But much of the new competition would be felt by existing producers outside the OECD area who will be replaced by the new producers with even lower costs, since the Trilateral countries have already ceased producing the goods in question. In order not to be suspected of understating the potential future threat to manufacturing industries which use substantial inputs of less-skilled labor, we have constructed—for the United States and Japan where that proved feasible—what might be called disaster scenarios in which all of manufacturing industry which uses less-skilled labor above a certain threshold in its total employment is wiped out by new competitors. Even then, the growth of export opportunities and what seem to us reasonable assumptions as to the substitution between different categories of labor will prevent the scenario from developing into disastrous consequences for the weaker part of the labor force.

There is clearly a discrepancy of major proportions between the alarmist views often expressed in the public debate and the conclusions of most economic analyses, including our study. It remains a major task for economists and the policymakers whom they advise to explain carefully and patiently that there is an important exaggeration in the proportions perceived in the public debate. The most fruitful line to take in this effort is not to deny there is a problem—a process of trade expansion does create both losers and winners—but to explain why efforts at correcting growing inequalities in the Trilateral countries should not be directed in any significant way towards restraining the growth of trade and foreign direct investment. Regardless of whether these flows in an increasingly globalized economy are responsible for only a minimal or a small, but still significant part of the deterioration of the relative position of less-skilled labor, it would be a mistake to attempt to slow down the process of globalization. There are more efficient ways of dealing with the implications of this process for the labor markets in the Trilateral countries. Growing trade and investment flows with the non-OECD area help to maintain competitive pressures which are essential to innovation and productivity gains in the Trilateral countries, while enlarging the range of consumer and intermediate products. In assessing the benefits to consumers from the availability of goods produced in low-cost countries, it should be recalled that cheap manufactured products are demanded in particular by low-income groups in our societies. In addition, the costs of protecting the jobs that might have continued to produce the goods in question will typically be high—sometimes more than average earnings in the sector of industry concerned. For example, the cost per job saved through textile quotas in the United States has been estimated at around US$40,000 or significantly above average earnings per worker in the industry. Protectionism is costly and inefficient.

The question of protectionism has been raised most recently in connection with proposals to impose labor standards in global trade. In the April 1996 G-7 employment meeting in Lille, France, the United States and France took up possible inclusion of labor standards in the agenda for the WTO Ministerial Meeting in Singapore in December 1996, in order to prevent so-called social dumping. This is a vague and dangerous notion which, if it could be implemented, would probably do harm to both the new low-cost producers and to the Trilateral countries.

The main reason for this characterization is that labor standards should diverge across countries which differ greatly in incomes, tastes, resources and skill endowments. Diversity in these respects provides a main source for mutually beneficial trade. The low-cost countries will find labor standards that raise their costs significantly dangerous to their competitive advantage in activities that use their ample less-skilled labor relatively intensively, while the Trilateral countries are likely to find inadequate any raising of global labor standards which does not check and ideally reverse their comparative disadvantage. There is probably only a limited basis for any multilaterally negotiated and mutually acceptable agreement between the two positions. There can be no objection, of course, to exploring such a basis covering fundamental rights such as non-discrimination, the principle of some health and safety standards and, maybe, the prohibition of forced labor. But any agreement would be likely to be weak in terms of enforceability, and deal only with the most egregious practices, hence leaving the signatories with a wide latitude. Nevertheless, maybe the pressure of such multilateral standards could in fact constrain protectionism because there would be less scope for countries to act unilaterally.

The proposal to impose labor standards in global trade has to be seen, maybe even primarily, as a step to protect the distribution of income in the Trilateral countries rather than as a measure to improve conditions for workers in the non-OECD area. As such it is clearly inferior to domestic reforms in the Trilateral countries designed to redress some of the observed growing inequalities which have affected the weaker parts of the labor force, but without setting up the wrong incentives.

In the long run the most efficient course of action is to upgrade the skills of the work force, hence gradually shifting the relative supply of skilled and less-skilled. Such a process has long been underway, but it has not kept pace with the shift in demand towards the skilled.

In the shorter run the focus has to be also on measures which change the relative price of skilled versus unskilled labor, in other words enlarge the scope for wage differentiation, since this will shift the demand for labor towards the less-skilled. But in order to preserve acceptable consumption possibilities for the latter, greater differentiation of wages should be accompanied by changes in tax and transfer systems which assure that the less-skilled are not left too far behind in the evolution of their disposable incomes.

In the United States, where wage flexibility is greater than elsewhere, this problem has been recognized to some extent through the introduction of the Earned Income Tax Credit (EITC), originally implemented under Presi-dent Carter and widened by President Reagan, but recently, unfortunately, attacked in the U.S. Congress. The EITC enlarges the consumption possibilities of the "working poor" and widens the difference between low wages and unemployment benefits, hence preserving an incentive to actively seek em-ployment. Some other countries, notably the United Kingdom (where wage flexibility is also considerable), have experimented with similar schemes.

In countries where the wage structure is more rigid, such as many European countries, there would appear to be a case for lowering the high indirect labor costs differentially so that these costs are reduced most sharply for the lowest-paid and then phased in gradually for those earning more. France is a recent example of a country that has moved in this direction by eliminating completely for those on the minimum wage indirect labor costs which amount to as much as 40 per cent of take-home pay. The experience is still too recent to evaluate, but the proposal seems well-designed to increase the relative demand for the less-skilled.

Finally, in countries where the wage structure is equally rigid but indirect labor costs leave less scope for significant reduction (because they are already modest), outright subsidies to employers hiring less-skilled workers within well-defined categories may be considered. Some European countries are experimenting with steps of this kind, particularly in personal services, where the high level of take-home pay has squeezed most of the earlier numerous jobs out of existence.

All of these initiatives share the feature of lowering the relative cost of employing less-skilled workers, hence encouraging the demand for them until changes in relative supply can bring about a more durable balance. They are all in some way a burden for the public finances and they will therefore have to be evaluated very carefully before implementation at a time when public sector deficits are already running at high levels. They are all based on the premise that it is better to be employed at a relatively low wage, supplemented by a tax credit or a more indirect form of subsidy, than to be unemployed, since the latter manifestation of inequality is the most onerous among the indications that the labor market is not functioning properly.

The challenge to the Trilateral countries does not lie therefore in seeking any direct response to the increasingly vigorous competition in a globalized economy by simply trying to limit active participation in it. Such a course of action would reduce welfare rather than enhance it. Rather, the task is to strengthen the capacity to adjust to change while both preserving the considerable net benefits of free trade and investment flows and temporarily compensating those who are initially most unfavorably affected by them.

SELECTED REFERENCES

Allais, Maurice. 1994. *Combats pour l'Europe*. Paris: Clément Juglar.

Arthuis, Jean. 1993. *Rapport d'Information sur l'Incidence Économique et Fiscale des Délocalisations hors du Territoire National des Activités Industrielles et de Service*. Paris: Sénat.

Baldwin, Robert. 1995. The Effects of Trade and Foreign Direct Investment on Employment and Relative Wages. *The OECD Jobs Study, Working Papers No. 4*. Paris: OECD.

Bhagwati, Jagdish. 1990. *Protectionism*. Cambridge, Mass.: MIT Press.

Bhagwati, Jagdish. 1994. Trade and the Wages of the Unskilled: Is Marx Striking Again? In *Trade and Wages*, ed. J. Bhagwati and M. Koster. Washington, D.C.: American Enterprise Institute.

Borjas, George J., Richard Freeman and Lawrence F. Katz. 1991. *On the Labor Market Effects of Immigration and Trade*. Harvard Institute of Economic Research Discussion Paper 1556. Cambridge, Mass.

Borjas, George J. and Valerie A. Ramey. 1993. *Foreign Competition, Market Power and Wage Inequality:Theory and Evidence*. National Bureau of Economic Research Working Paper 4556. Cambridge, Mass.: NBER.

Bound, John and George Johnson. 1992. Changes in the Structure of Wages in the 1980s: An Evaluation of Alternative Explanations. *American Economic Review* 82: 371-92.

Buigues, Pierre-André and Alexis Jacquemin. 1995. Les Échages Commerciaus entre les Pays à Bas Salaires et l'Union Européenne. *Économie Internationale* 84: 61-80. Paris: Centre d'Études Prospectives et d'Informations Internationales.

Burtless, Gary. 1995. International Trade and the Rise in Earnings Inequality. *Journal of Economic Literature* 33 (2): 800-16.

Card, David and Richard B. Freeman. 1994. Small Differences That Matter: Canada vs. the United States. In *Working Under Different Rules*, ed. Richard B. Freeman, 189-222. A National Bureau of Economic Research Project Report. New York: Russell Sage Foundation.

Cooper, Richard N. 1994. *Foreign Trade, Wages and Unemployment*. Harvard University Department of Economics Working Paper. Cambridge, Mass.

Cortes, Olivier, Sebatien Jean and Jean Pisani-Ferry. 1995. Trade with Emerging Countries and the Labour Markets: The French Case. Unpublished paper for CEPII/ECARE Workshop. Paris.

Deardorff, Alan and Robert Staiger. 1988. An Interpretation of the Factor Content of Trade. *Journal of International Economics* 24: 93-107.

Drèze, Jacques and Henri Snessens. 1994. Technical Development, Competition from Low-Wage Economies and Low-Skilled Employment. *Swedish Economic Policy Review* 1:185-214.

Economic Planning Agency. 1995. *Economic Survey of Japan*. Tokyo: Ministry of Finance Printing Office.

Feenstra, Robert C. and Gordon H. Hanson. 1995. Globalization, Outsourcing and Wage Inequality. Unpublished manuscript. University of California at Davis.

de Fontenay, Patrick, Georgio Gomel and Eduard Hochreiter, eds. 1995. *Western Europe in Transition: The Impact of the Opening up of Eastern Europe and the Former Soviet Union.* Banca d'Italia, International Monetary Fund, Oesterreichische Nationalbank.

Freeman, Richard B. 1995. Are Your Wages Set in Beijing? *Journal of Economic Perspectives* 9 (3): 15-32.

Freeman, Richard B. and Ana Revenga. 1995. How Much Has LDC Trade Affected Western Job Markets? Unpublished paper for CEPII/CARE Workshop. Paris.

Goldsmith, Sir James. 1993. *The Trap.* New York: Carroll and Graf.

Goldsmith, Sir James. 1995. *The Response.* London: Macmillan.

Hamermesh, Daniel. 1986. The Demand for Labor in the Long Run. In *Handbook of Labor Economics,* ed. Orley Ashenfelter and Richard Layard, 429-71. Amsterdam: Elsevier Science Publishers.

International Labour Organization. 1995. *World Employment 1995.* Geneva: ILO

Johnson, George E. and Frank P. Stafford. 1993 January 5-7. International Competition and Real Wages. In *American Economic Association Meetings.*

Katz, Lawrence and Kevin Murphy. 1992. Changes in Relative Wages in the United States, 1963-87: Supply and Demand Factors. *Quarterly Journal of Economics* 107: 35-78.

Katz, Lawrence F. and Lawrence H. Summers. 1989. Industry Rents: Evidence and Implications. *Brookings Papers on Microeconomic Activity,* 209-291. Washington, D. C.: Brookings Institution.

Krueger, Alan B. 1993. How Computers Have Changed the Wage Structure: Evidence from Microdata, 1984-1989. *The Quarterly Journal of Economics.* Cambridge, Mass.

Krueger, Alan B. 1995. Labor Market Shifts and the Price Puzzle Revisited. Mimeo. Princeton University.

Krugman, Paul. 1995a. Growing World Trade: Causes and Consequences. *Brookings Papers on Economic Activity* 1:327-77 (with comments by Richard Cooper and T. N. Srinavasan). Washington, D. C.: Brookings Institution.

Krugman, Paul. 1995b. *Technology, Trade and Factor Prices.* National Bureau of Economic Research Working Paper 5355. Cambridge, Mass.: NBER.

Krugman, Paul. 1995c. *Technology, Trade and Factor Prices.* Stanford University, Mimeo.

Larre, Benedicte. 1995. The Impact of Trade on Labour Markets: An Analysis by Industry. *The OECD Jobs Study, Working Papers No. 6.* Paris: OECD.

Lawrence, Robert Z. 1996a. *Single World Divided Nations: International Trade and OECD Labor Markets.* Washington, D.C.: Brookings Institution and OECD Development Centre.

Lawrence, Robert Z. 1996b. The Slow Growth Mystery. *Foreign Affairs* 75 (1): 146-152.

Lawrence, Robert Z. and Matthew J. Slaughter. 1993. Trade and U.S. Wages: Great Sucking Sound or Small Hiccup? *Brookings Papers on Microeconomic Activity* 2:161-226. Washington, D.C.: Brookings Institution.

Lawrence, Robert Z. and Carolyn Evans. 1996. *Trade and Wages: Insights from the Crystal Ball*. National Bureau of Economic Research Working Paper 5633. Cambridge, Mass: NBER

Leamer, Edward E. 1994. *Trade, Wages and Revolving Door Ideas*. National Bureau of Economic Research Working Paper 4716. Cambridge, Mass.: NBER.

Leamer, Edward E. 1995. *The Heckscher-Ohlin Model in Theory and Practice*. Princeton Studies in International Finance 77. Princeton.

Leamer, Edward E. 1996. A Trial Economist's View of U.S. Wages and Globalization. In *Imports, Exports and the American Worker*, ed. Susan Collins. Washington D.C.: Brookings Institution.

Meissner, Doris M., Robert D. Hormats, Antonio Garrigues Walker and Shijuro Ogata. 1993. *International Migration Challenges in a New Era*. A Report to the Trilateral Commission 44. New York: Trilateral Commission.

Messerlin, Patrick A. 1995. The Impact of Trade and Foreign Direct Investment on Labour Markets: The French Case. *The OECD Jobs Study, Working Papers No. 9*. Paris: OECD.

Minford, Patrick et al. 1995. *The Elixir of Growth: Trade, Non-Traded Goods and Development*. Centre for Economic Policy Research Discussion Paper 1165. London: CEPR.

Nakamura, Yoshiaki and Ninoru Shibuya. 1995. *The Closedness of the Japanese Markets: A Critical Review of Econometric Studies*. Studies in International Trade and Industry 20. Tokyo: Research Institute of International Trade and Industry.

Nikkeiren. 1994. *"Sin Nihon teki Keiei Sisutemu nado Kenkyu Purojekuto" ni kansuru Anketo Chosa Hokoku*, (Report on Survey made in relation with the Study Project on New Japanese Management System). August. Tokyo: Nihon Keieisha Dantai Renmei (Japan Federation of Employers' Associations).

OECD. 1994. *Jobs Study*. Vols. I-II. Paris: OECD.

OECD. 1995. *Global Interdependence: Links Between the OECD Countries and the Main Developing Economies*. Paris: OECD.

Otake, Fumio. 1994. 1980 Nendai no Shotoku Shisan Bumpai (Income and Asset Distribution in the 1980s). *The Economic Studies Quarterly* 45 (5). December. Tokyo: Japan Association of Economics and Econometrics.

Ravegna, Ana L. 1992. Exporting Jobs? The Impact of Import Competition on Employment and Wages in U.S. Manufacturing. *Quarterly Journal of Economics* 107 (1): 255-82.

Ricardo, David. 1817. *On the Principles of Political Economy and Taxation*. London: Reprint by Penguin, Harmoudsworth, 1971.

Richardson, J. David. 1995. Income Inequality and Trade: How to Think, What to Conclude. *Journal of Economic Perspectives* 9 (3): 33-55

Sachs, Jeffrey O. and Howard J. Shatz. 1994. Trade and Jobs in U.S. Manufacturing. *Brookings Papers on Economic Activity*. Washington, D.C.: Brookings Institution.

Shakai Keizai Seisansei Honbu. 1994. *Howaito Kara no Seisansei ni kansuru Chosa Hokokusho* (Report on Productivity of White-collar Workers). June. Tokyo.

Slaughter, Matthew J. 1994. The Impact of Internationalization on U.S. Income Distribution. In *Finance and the International Economy 8: The Amex Bank Review Prize Essays*, ed. Richard O'Brien, 143-158. New York: Oxford University Press, 1994.

Stolper, Wolfgang and Paul A. Samuelson. 1941. Protection and Real Wages. *Review of Economics and Statistics* 9: 58-73

Tachibanaki, Toshiaki ed. 1992. *Satei, Shoshin, Chinginkettei* (Valuation, Promotion and Wages). Tokyo: Yuhikaku.

Tachibanaki, Toshiaki et al. 1995. *Nihon no Yushutsunyu to Koyo Chingin* (Foreign Trade, Employment, and Wages in Japan). Discussion Paper #95-DOJ-62. Tokyo: Research Institute of International Trade and Industry.

Wood, Adrian. 1994. *North-South Trade, Employment and Inequality: Changing Fortunes in a Skill-Driven World*. Oxford: Clarendon Press.

Wood, Adrian. 1995. How Trade Hurt Unskilled Workers. *Journal of Economic Perspectives* 9 (3): 57-80.

World Bank. 1995a. *Global Economic Prospects and the Developing Countries*. Washington D.C.: IBRD.

World Bank. 1995b. *The Employment Crisis in Industrial Countries: Is International Integration to Blame?* Regional Perspectives on World Development Report 1995. Washington D.C.: IBRD.

World Bank. 1995c. *Workers in an Integrating World*. World Development Report 1995. New York: Oxford University Press.

Yamagami, Toshihiko. 1993. Howaito Kara no Seisansei (Productivity of White-collar Workers). *Sumi Sei Soken Repoto*. October. Tokyo.

Yamagami, Toshihiko. 1994. Gokai darakeno Howaito Kara no Seisansei (Productivity of White-collar Workers Totally Misunderstood). *Syukan Toyo Keizai*. August 6. Tokyo.

Yashiro, Naohiro. 1995a. Koyo Mondai wo Kangaeru (Issues in Employment). In *Keizai Seisaku no Kangae Kata* (Introduction to Economic Policy), ed. Masahiro Kawai, Takehiko Musashi, and Naohiro Yashiro. December. Tokyo: Yuhikaku.

Yashiro, Naohiro. 1995b. *Keiki Kotai to Kigyo nai Kajo Koyo* (Labor-hoarding in the Japanese Firms in Recession Periods). Japan Center for Economic Researcy Discussion Paper 37. September. Tokyo: JCER.